NEW DIRECTIONS FOR ADULT AND CONTINUING EDUCATION

Susan Imel, *Ohio State University*
EDITOR-IN-CHIEF

The Welfare-to-Work Challenge for Adult Literacy Educators

Larry G. Martin
University of Wisconsin-Milwaukee

James C. Fisher
University of Wisconsin-Milwaukee

EDITORS

Number 83, Fall 1999

JOSSEY-BASS PUBLISHERS
San Francisco

THE WELFARE-TO-WORK CHALLENGE FOR ADULT LITERACY EDUCATORS
Larry G. Martin, James C. Fisher (eds.)
New Directions for Adult and Continuing Education, no. 83
Susan Imel, Editor-in-Chief

Microfilm copies of issues and articles are available in 16mm and 35mm, as well as microfiche in 105mm, through University Microfilms Inc., 300 North Zeeb Road, Ann Arbor, Michigan 48106-1346.

ISSN 1052-2891   ISBN 0-7879-1170-4

NEW DIRECTIONS FOR ADULT AND CONTINUING EDUCATION is part of The Jossey-Bass Higher and Adult Education Series and is published quarterly by Jossey-Bass Inc., Publishers, 350 Sansome Street, San Francisco, California 94104-1342. Periodicals postage paid at San Francisco, California, and at additional mailing offices. Postmaster: Send address changes to New Directions for Adult and Continuing Education, Jossey-Bass Inc., Publishers, 350 Sansome Street, San Francisco, California 94104-1342.

SUBSCRIPTIONS cost $58.00 for individuals and $104.00 for institutions, agencies, and libraries.

EDITORIAL CORRESPONDENCE should be sent to the Editor-in-Chief, Susan Imel, ERIC/ACVE, 1900 Kenny Road, Columbus, Ohio 43210-1090. E-mail: imel.1@osu.edu.

Cover photograph by Wernher Krutein/PHOTOVAULT © 1990.

Jossey-Bass Web address: http://www.josseybass.com

Printed in the United States of America on acid-free recycled paper containing 100 percent recovered waste paper, of which at least 20 percent is postconsumer waste.

CONTENTS

EDITORS' NOTES

Attempting to describe the characteristics of the welfare-to-work movement, to say nothing of its impact on adult basic education and literacy programs across the country, is like aiming at fifty different moving targets that, although similar in significant ways, possess their own unique speed and dimensions. The laws and policies driving this movement have been and are being developed at both the federal and the state level. These laws and policies, as well as the political environments that produce them, vary between these levels of government and across the fifty states, and they change very frequently. Given the variations in policy and the speed of change in this area, some of what is now in print on this topic is already obsolete. The authors and editors of this journal hope it will become an integral part of the important discourse about the role and promise of adult basic education in the wake of dramatic welfare reform.

Notwithstanding the daily policy changes in this area, a somewhat consistent conceptual framework, consisting of several important assumptions, seems to be emerging regarding the transition from welfare to work. As a way of introducing the reader to the articles that follow, we identify here some of the assumptions that undergird the welfare-to-work movement:

- Work is the principal mechanism for advancement in our society. (This is a substantial change from an earlier assumption that education is the most vital mechanism for achieving advancement.)
- Welfare recipients will not avail themselves of work opportunities unless they are forced to do so; consequently, a graduated system of rewards and punishments is the most effective approach to motivate them to acquire and maintain employment.
- Welfare recipients with low literacy skills who are generally inexperienced or unsuccessful with education will on their own pursue the education needed for workplace advancement.
- The most important activity for single parents (mainly mothers) is full-time work outside the home, rather than full-time parenting.
- Employers will provide the education necessary to prepare unskilled former welfare recipients for advancement beyond the entry level.
- Preparing former welfare recipients for the workplace provides an appropriate context, by itself, for teaching basic literacy skills.
- Employment opportunities exist, especially at the entry level, for former welfare recipients.
- Employment immunizes former welfare recipients from future economic downturns.

These assumptions are examined in the various chapters of this source-book. In Chapter One, Elisabeth Hayes reviews important federal and state legislation and the maze of policy interpretations surrounding the welfare-to-work movement. In Chapter Two, Barbara Sparks examines critical cultural and economic issues that affect the welfare-to-work transition. Specifically, she discusses three dilemmas that emerge for practitioners and those employed in adult literacy and basic education programs.

In Chapter Three, James C. Fisher examines four strands of research that inform welfare-to-work policies and illuminate the effects of this research on the conceptualization and delivery of adult literacy education. The studies Fisher cites describe participant characteristics, program characteristics, program goals, and program outcomes. In Chapter Four, Larry Martin defines the parameters of the traditional academic model of literacy program development and explores three alternative approaches that could more effectively help welfare recipients move into the workplace.

Chapter Five focuses on delivering adult literacy education in the workplace. The authors, Eunice N. Askov and Edward E. Gordon, describe and analyze the kind of workplace learning needed for a welfare-to-work transition. In Chapter Six, Daniel V. Folkman and Kalyani Rai take the reader from the workplace to the community, examining how community-based literacy programs are responding to the welfare-to-work transition and discussing the roles and functions of community-based agencies in the wake of these changes.

In Chapter Seven, John M. Dirkx discusses the impact of the welfare-to-work movement on the role of the practitioner. Dirkx considers the new skill sets that may be required for practitioners, as well as the necessary changes in staff development and preparation. Finally, in the Epilogue we identify important issues raised by the authors and explore future directions for study, practice, and research.

We believe that this overview of current research and practice will help both academicians and practitioners better understand this dynamic policy area and develop appropriate responses for a variety of situations and clients.

James C. Fisher
Larry G. Martin
Editors

JAMES C. FISHER is associate professor of adult and continuing education at the University of Wisconsin-Milwaukee.

LARRY G. MARTIN is associate professor of adult and continuing education and department chair at the University of Wisconsin-Milwaukee.

1

This chapter discusses federal and state legislation that affects the planning, funding, implementation, and evaluation of adult literacy programs.

Policy Issues That Drive the Transformation of Adult Literacy

Elisabeth Hayes

In the last few years we have witnessed tremendous changes in policies shaping the welfare system, changes that have significant implications for adult literacy education (ALE). Under the banner of "ending welfare as we know it," policymakers have adopted a "Work First" approach that emphasizes economic self-sufficiency and moving welfare recipients into the workforce as quickly as possible. For the most part, education (particularly ALE) in this environment—when it is considered at all—has been reduced to short-term programs for those not yet employed or, for those who do manage to acquire a job, limited after-work training sessions. The drop in educational participation among welfare recipients has been dramatic. For example, from 1994 to 1997, participation rates of California welfare recipients dropped from 76.7 percent to 53.3 percent; in Wisconsin, participation rates dropped from 60.4 percent to 12.5 percent (Strawn, 1998b).

This situation is particularly troublesome given the low education and skill levels of most welfare recipients. The 1992 National Adult Literacy Survey (NALS) found that 50 percent of welfare recipients were at the lowest level of literacy (Barton and Jenkins, 1995). It is estimated that 25 to 40 percent of welfare recipients have learning disabilities (Cohen, 1998). According to the U.S. Department of Labor (1998), almost half of all welfare recipients lack a high school credential, and almost two-thirds of long-term recipients lack a diploma. These statistics are based on the welfare population before the recent drops in the welfare rolls; individuals remaining in the welfare system are now even more likely to have limited skills and education. For example, in Wisconsin, the percentage of welfare participants with a high school credential dropped from 51 percent in 1995 to 17 percent in 1998 (Governor's Wisconsin Works Education and Training Committee, 1998). It is estimated that 80 percent of those left on cash assistance have less than a fifth-grade reading level (Huston, 1998).

The lack of emphasis on education in current welfare policy is based on evidence that basic education and training programs, by themselves, are ineffective at moving people off welfare and into work. However, research shows that strategies concentrating on moving people into jobs quickly are effective only at helping more welfare recipients find work, not at increasing their wages and moving them out of poverty. Programs with the greatest long-term impact on employment and advancement have been those that combine skills development with strategies that move people into jobs more rapidly (Strawn, 1998a). A National Governors' Association (1998) report stressed the need for states to combine "quick employment" strategies with basic education instruction in a work-focused context. However, the role of ALE remains peripheral and ill-defined in many policies.

In this chapter I review key federal and state legislation affecting ALE and describe policy interpretation and implementation issues at the local level. The limited length of this chapter precluded a comprehensive analysis of state and local policies, and the examples I have selected are meant to be suggestive of key issues, not representative of all policies and concerns.

The Federal Context

Since the mid-1990s and the advent of the "Republican Revolution" (Gold, 1998), federal legislation has increasingly reflected a policy approach called the New Federalism. As Watson and Gold (1998) explain, New Federalism is characterized by devolution, which includes passing policy responsibilities from the federal government to state and local governments. This approach is reflected in block grants to states, reduced federal aid, and greater flexibility granted to states in implementing federal policies. The assumption underlying devolution is that state and local governments can be more responsive and effective than the federal government at meeting the needs of their constituencies.

Several federal legislative acts that embody New Federalism provided the basis for welfare reform and shaped the current role of ALE. The Personal Responsibility and Work Opportunity Reconciliation Act of 1996 and the 1997 Welfare-to-Work Program established new requirements for welfare receipt and placed restrictions on recipients' educational participation. The Workforce Investment Act of 1998 affects the funding, coordination, and evaluation of federally funded adult literacy programs. In this section I briefly describe the elements of these acts that have the most significant implications for the provision of ALE.

Personal Responsibility and Work Opportunity Reconciliation Act. The Personal Responsibility and Work Opportunity Reconciliation Act (PRWORA) of 1996 reformed the nation's welfare laws and instituted the

Temporary Assistance for Needy Families (TANF) system for providing block grants to states. This legislation includes provisions that increase the pressure on states and localities to move people into work. The new laws include a twenty-four-month time limit for welfare recipients to find work or begin participating in a "work activity." There is also a new lifetime eligibility limit, of five years, for all welfare recipients. To receive full TANF funding, states must meet minimum federal requirements for work participation rates of their welfare recipients. There are two main requirements: a certain percentage of welfare recipients must be placed into jobs or engaged in an allowable work activity, and recipients must work a prescribed number of hours each week. The legislation requires states to gradually increase the percentage of recipients participating in work activities and increase the number of hours recipients work per week over the five-year period from 1997 to 2002. For example, in 1997 states were required to demonstrate a 25 percent work participation rate for one-parent families, with a minimum of twenty hours of work activities per week. In 2002, the requirements increase to a 50 percent work participation rate for single-parent families, with a minimum of thirty hours of work activities per week.

PRWORA defines work activities that count toward the first twenty hours of the work participation rate (or the first thirty hours for two-parent families). In addition to actual employment, these work activities can include certain education and training activities. These include job searching (only for six weeks and not for more than four consecutive weeks); on-the-job training, work experience, or community service; vocational education (for a maximum of twelve months, and only for a maximum of 30 percent of those included in the work participation rate); and secondary school or the equivalent, or education directly related to employment, but only for participants under the age of twenty.

PRWORA also identifies education and training activities that may count toward work participation after the minimum twenty (or thirty) hours are reached. These activities include job skills training directly related to employment, education directly related to employment (but only for those without a high school diploma or GED), and secondary school or GED classes for those who have not received a high school diploma. Finally, PRWORA specifies activities that can be funded through the TANF block grant program but do not meet PRWORA's work participation requirements. These include adult literacy and basic education classes, English as a second language (ESL) classes, and postsecondary education.

ALE would seem to have a very limited place in the provisions of this legislation. However, several points are worth noting. First, states have considerable leeway in how they define certain activities in the first category of allowable work activities, including work experience, community service, and vocational education. States might choose to include ALE in their definition of these activities. States conceivably could include ALE as one of the second category of activities that count beyond the minimum participation rates. For example, ALE might be considered education directly related to employment. Also, ALE can be funded by TANF even when it is not included as an allowable work activity. With many states experiencing reduced caseloads and surplus funds, more money could be made available for literacy programming, at least in theory.

PRWORA was the starting point for current welfare-related policies; subsequent legislation has modified its provisions and added new programs. This ongoing policy development makes it even more difficult to understand and implement the new regulations, an issue addressed later in the chapter. The following legislation represents one of the first additions to PRWORA.

The Department of Labor's 1997 Welfare-to-Work Program. The Welfare-to-Work (WtW) program, administered by the U.S. Department of Labor, was created through an amendment to the Balanced Budget Act of 1997. This legislation makes funds available to states for activities that "move and keep individuals in lasting unsubsidized employment" (Knell, 1998). Eligible activities include job readiness training; actual employment opportunities, to provide people with work experience; job placement services; and postemployment services. Basic skills training and ESL instruction are included as eligible postemployment activities. The program provides funds to qualifying states through both formula and competitive grants. Not less than 70 percent of the participants in programs funded through both kinds of grants must be burdened with at least two of three specified barriers to employment. One such barrier is not having a high school or equivalency diploma *and* having low reading or math skills. The competitive grants are targeted in particular toward moving participants who are "least job ready" into jobs.

The WtW program offers literacy educators a potentially larger role and more funds than TANF does. However, under both programs the role of ALE efforts has shifted away from preparing people for employment and toward providing instruction concurrent with employment. This shift has significant implications for how literacy educators conceptualize their role in moving people from welfare to work, including the need for them to collaborate much more closely with employers.

The Workforce Investment Act of 1998. This act includes Title II The Adult Education and Family Literacy Act, replacing the Adult Education Act and the National Literacy Act as a basis for federal funding and oversight of adult literacy programs. Although this legislation is not explicitly linked to welfare reform, it has strong philosophical ties to welfare legislation. Perhaps most notable is that ALE is included as a part of employment and training legislation, not educational legislation, thereby reinforcing its connection to work. However, Title II does retain broad educational purposes for ALE: to help adults become literate and obtain the knowledge and skills necessary for employment and self-sufficiency, to help adults who are parents obtain the educational skills necessary to become full partners in the educational development of their children, and to help adults complete their high school education. A significant element of Title II is the specification of core performance indicators that will be used to evaluate state and local programs. Three core indicators are as follows (USWorkforce.org, 1998):

1. Demonstrated improvements in literacy skill levels
2. Placement in, retention in, or completion of postsecondary education, training, unsubsidized employment, or career advancement
3. Receipt of a secondary school diploma or its equivalent

The states negotiate performance levels for each indicator with the secretary of labor and may add additional indicators. States are required to allocate funding based on programs' performance in relation to these indicators. Accordingly, the legislation puts more pressure on literacy providers receiving federal funds to demonstrate "measurable" program outcomes. The overall Workforce Investment Act promotes the collaboration of literacy providers with other educational agencies and employment services through the creation of one-stop delivery systems that give participants access to a wide range of programs. Although such collaboration is not a new concept, the act establishes more formal criteria and procedures for such systems.

State Legislative Initiatives

As noted above, PRWORA and WtW give states some flexibility in determining how and when to use ALE in meeting federal requirements. There is considerable variation in how states have developed their own welfare legislation and how this legislation affects ALE. Although most states have made their policies available through Web sites and public documents, these are often broad statements that do not include, for example, how states are defining activities such as vocational education or education related to employment (which may or may not include ALE). Even when I spoke directly with researchers and policy analysts monitoring welfare reform at the national level, or with educators and state staff in various states, I often encountered uncertainty about state policies and literacy education in particular. In the push to move people into work, many states have made education within welfare reform a secondary consideration. Here I note a few general ways in which state policies have implications for ALE.

A 1997 summary of state TANF plans (National Governors' Association, 1997) highlights policy differences across states. Although the summary does not mention education specifically, some of the policy variations it describes can potentially affect welfare recipients' access to ALE. For example, although federal law places a lifetime limit of five years on welfare benefits for each individual, states may exempt up to 20 percent of their monthly caseload from this limit. States may also have shorter time limits than federal law requires, periodic time limits, work activity limits, and conditional time limits, in which continued receipt of benefits is based on criteria such as a disability that prevents employment. Although federal law requires recipients to engage in work, as defined by the state, within twenty-four months of receiving assistance, states may require recipients to obtain work earlier than this. At the time of the National Governors' Association report, twenty-one states required participants to find employment less than twenty-four months after receiving assistance. These shorter limits on lifetime receipt of benefits and work requirements add greater pressure to move people into jobs, further relegating literacy education to the margins.

Many states initiated welfare reform strategies prior to PRWORA through federal waivers, creating additional diversity in policies. Most states continued the policies authorized under this waiver system, which may be inconsistent with national legislation (National Governors' Association, 1997). Some waivers allow states to place greater emphasis on literacy education. A notable example is Tennessee's Families First program, in which welfare recipients who read at less than a ninth-grade level are exempted from the work participation requirement and the five-year time limit on benefits, until their reading improves. To maintain the exemption, such recipients are required to enroll in a GED program for a minimum of twenty hours per week and demonstrate satisfactory progress toward achieving the required reading proficiency (White, Ziegler, and Bingham, 1998). Other examples include the Texas CHOICES program, which designates ALE an allowable work activity as part of the state's waiver of federal requirements. State waivers do not always produce more lenient policies, however, and in some states they place even greater restrictions on recipients' educational options than do the federal requirements.

States can also use their own funding to provide support for welfare recipients, thereby exempting them from federal work participation requirements and time limits on benefits and, presumably, increasing their opportunities for education. For instance, the Illinois TANF program allows participants who work twenty-five hours per week to stop the federal five-year time clock while still receiving benefits, because the cash assistance is paid entirely from state funds. Educational services are available to these participants beyond their twenty-five hours of work. There is some flexibility in how work participation requirements can be met, and literacy education can be part of approved activities. For example, vocational training as an approved activity can include GED preparation or basic skills training, as long as these make up less than half of the training hours (J. Muller, Illinois State Board of Education, personal communication, October 14, 1998). Unfortunately, caseworkers are strongly encouraged to steer clients to work rather than education, an issue I discuss in the next section.

As the number of welfare recipients drops, the role of education in welfare reform is receiving more attention from state policymakers. Another report from the National Governors' Association (1998) focused on strategies for integrating education with employment, to assist the career development of low-skilled workers. In Wisconsin, the governor recently convened a committee to make recommendations on the role of education and training in the Wisconsin Works (W–2) program (Governor's Wisconsin Works Education and Training Committee, 1998). This renewed interest in education is due to at least two factors. First, as caseloads are reduced and welfare recipients move into the workforce, states are faced with the problem of ensuring that former welfare recipients stay employed and move into positions that offer "family-supporting" wages. A growing number of states are investing in postemployment services for welfare recipients and for the "working poor" who are not receiving assistance. The WtW program designates funds specifically for these activities, and ALE is a "fundable" activity under this program. Second, the remaining welfare population faces considerable challenges in securing employment, including learning disabilities and poor skills. There is growing interest in strategies to provide appropriate job placement and support for these individuals. In the first round of WtW funding, seven states requested WtW grants to develop program models for welfare recipients with learning disabilities (National Institute for Literacy, 1998).

The examples of Tennessee and other states with more liberal policies regarding literacy education may be particularly informative given the need to provide greater educational opportunities to current and former welfare recipients. In describing the creation of Tennessee's Families First program, White, Ziegler, and Bingham (1998) note that state legislators and state departments of human services had a limited understanding of the needs of less educated adults. The involvement of adult educators, particularly those who had experience with the earlier JOBSWORK program, was a critical factor in shaping the educational elements of the state legislation. Reports of adult education students to the task force were part of an effort to educate policymakers about the benefits of literacy education. One legislator became a mentor for two welfare mothers and described how this experience led to his efforts to increase the grade-level criteria for employability from 5.9 to 8.9. Such an example suggests the impact that adult educators can have if they take a more active role in educating policymakers about the educational needs of current and former welfare recipients.

Local Policy Interpretation and Implementation Issues

State policies often leave considerable leeway for interpretation at the local level. The "Work First" emphasis of current welfare policy means educational options often are ignored or misunderstood by local social service providers. In many cases, welfare recipients are required to find employment as quickly as possible, with no educational options even considered until their job searches prove unsuccessful. In some places there is an emphasis on "applicant diversion," an effort to reduce the number of people receiving benefits by helping applicants find resources from other agencies and requiring them to engage in a job search during the application process. Few, if any, guidelines may be given to caseworkers to determine if applicants are employable. A critic of the New York City program (Krueger, 1998) points out that New York City seems to rely on a "labor market test of employability," meaning that a person is employable if he or she can find a job. There is no consideration of whether a person has the skills to move beyond entry-level jobs with subsistence-level wages. A follow-up survey of current and former welfare recipients in Milwaukee found that 38 percent of recipients determined to be ready for immediate entry into jobs had not completed high school. The majority who found work were placed in low-skill jobs paying wages at or below the poverty level and did not receive any training in higher-skill occupations. In a companion survey, employers indicated that even many low-skill jobs require basic reading, math, and computer skills; the majority of employers required that applicants for unskilled jobs have high school diplomas (Institute for Wisconsin's Future, 1998). Clearly, the skills and education of welfare recipients being referred to employers do not meet those employers' expectations, and recipients are not gaining access to additional training.

Typically even those individuals who are not considered to be job ready are required to engage in "work activities" as quickly as possible. This work-first-for-all approach is more stringent than the federal guidelines for work participation, which require that only a percentage of a state's caseload be engaged in work activities (currently just 30 percent of single-parent families) and subject only a percentage of participants to the five-year time limit (up to 20 percent of a state's caseload may be exempted). Some states and local districts have established stricter guidelines. However, in general the Work First mentality has obscured the opportunities within existing policies for at least a percentage of participants to be engaged in some alternative to work, such as education and training, for longer periods of time.

Another issue concerns the format and delivery of education for welfare recipients. Often social service providers as well as educators do not realize that policies allow for some flexibility in how recipients use their allowable hours of education. For example, in Wisconsin many providers do not realize that state policy allows educational hours to be aggregated in short-term education and training programs for recipients in certain employment categories. As an illustration, Wisconsin recipients placed in community service jobs (CSJs) can count ten hours of education and training per week as an allowable work activity. A person in a six-month CSJ placement can potentially accrue a total of 258 educational hours. He or she could use all these hours "up front," by participating in a training program for twenty-four hours per week for the first eleven weeks of the CSJ placement (in addition to work experience hours), to prepare for a more highly skilled job placement (Governor's Wisconsin Works Education and Training Committee, 1998). This aggregation of educational hours may allow literacy educators to provide more intensive instruction to participants prior to job placement, potentially helping them be more successful at meeting job demands once they move into employment.

Given the limited amount of time currently allocated to education, determining the content of educational programs presents some dilemmas. If literacy education is considered to be "education related to work," how can and should this be interpreted? Does this mean literacy educators should teach job-specific literacy skills, such as reading blueprints or writing a work order? Many employers are citing the development of "soft skills," such as punctuality, politeness, or even a work ethic, as the major educational need. Should literacy educators make these skills the focus of their programming, or does this approach simply meet the needs of employers for compliant workers, without helping learners develop abilities that will truly enable them to gain more power and autonomy in their lives? Would it be of greater benefit to help welfare recipients earn high school credentials, since credentials are a critical factor in increasing earnings and upward career mobility? Should literacy educators help welfare recipients learn family literacy skills, to help their children be more successful educationally and vocationally? Or should educators help students learn to confront issues like wage inequities, racism in hiring and promotion, or unsafe working conditions? One of the biggest concerns is finding ways to help participants develop the ability to support themselves economically before they reach the end of their limit on benefits.

Another set of issues concerns those individuals who have the most limited educational levels, poor basic skills, and the least work experience. For the most part, current policies do not account for the educational needs of this population, which may need long-term basic education to become employable at more than subsistence wages. Is "self-sufficiency" a reasonable short-term goal for such individuals? What expectations for student outcomes should be placed on educational programs that serve such learners, particularly given the new requirements for demonstrating a certain level of program performance? These individuals include a high proportion of adults with learning disabilities as well as other barriers to learning. This group also includes people with limited English skills. A *New York Times* article (Swarns, 1998) reported that since 1995, although the number of white single mothers on welfare in New York City has dropped 57 percent, the number of Hispanic single mothers on welfare dropped only 7 percent. Hispanics now make up 59 percent of the city's welfare recipients. Without additional funding and expertise, programs may not be equipped to meet the needs of these students. In the case of New York City, ESL classes have filled so rapidly that many Hispanics do not have access to instruction. In addition, many job training programs cannot accommodate students with limited English skills. Although city officials are now scrambling to fund additional programs for this population, the question remains whether these programs will be sufficient to meet the existing need and whether these women will ever be able to achieve self-sufficiency given current limits on education and training.

Future Directions

Legislation linked to welfare reform and ALE is still evolving. In the few months between the first and second drafts of this chapter, President Clinton proposed new initiatives to expand the provision of ALE and other education and training to improve the skills of workers. Adult literacy educators soon may find that they are no longer at the margins of welfare reform.

To take advantage of new policies, as well as to work more effectively with existing ones, literacy educators must take a proactive stance in seeking out information about legislation. This requires communicating with county and local human service agencies as well as state agencies, since many policies are subject to local interpretation. Just as critical is the need for literacy educators to be more involved in how policies are interpreted and implemented at the local level. Some literacy educators are taking on the role of educating caseworkers and employers about the educational alternatives allowable under current policies. Advocacy groups have been formed in some states to influence policymaking decisions as well as to inform welfare recipients about their educational options. For example, in Illinois, state regulations stipulate that an individual who does not have a high school diploma or who reads below the ninth-grade level is entitled to go to school for two years without working at the same time. Local welfare offices are either uninformed about this policy or are not informing clients of this option. Advocacy groups have begun to provide recipients with forms they can use to request a literacy test and to appeal activity plans that do not permit them to pursue education.

Building stronger networks for sharing information and strategies can be a potent way for literacy educators to take a more proactive stance in policy reform and implementation. The National Institute for Literacy (NIFL) supports a number of listservs for such conversations, most notably the National Literacy Advocacy Forum (see the NIFL Web site at http://novel.nifl.gov).

In this chapter I have taken an implicit stance that literacy educators should strive to understand welfare policies so as to become more involved in the new system. However, I end by questioning whether educators' increased involvement will support a system that is not in the best interests of their students or society. Current policies are aimed at ending welfare, not ending poverty. Some critics suggest that the current reform will increase the number of people, particularly children and single mothers, who live in poverty. Advocates of a "human capital" approach argue for greater investment in education as a long-term solution to poverty, along with reform of an economic system that supports a growing gap between the rich and poor. As literacy educators, should we support the Work First approach or challenge it? Some might claim that our only choice is to support the system, as long as we are dependent on public funding for our programs. In contrast, I would argue that literacy educators can assume a greater role as advocates for more informed policies. We face the challenge of educating ourselves about policies and their implications so that we may better educate policymakers and the public about important issues. We may find that political literacy has become a basic skill for literacy educators, as well as for those we serve.

References

Barton, P., and Jenkins, L. *Literacy and Dependency: The Literacy Skills of Welfare Recipients in the United States.* Princeton, N.J.: Educational Testing Service, 1995.

Cohen, M. "Education and Training Under Welfare Reform." *Welfare Information Network Issue Notes,* March 1998 [http://www.welfareinfo.org/edissue.htm].

Gold, S. *Issues Raised by the New Federalism.* Washington, D.C.: The Urban Institute, 1998 [http://newfederalism.urban.org/html/ntj.htm].

Governor's Wisconsin Works Education and Training Committee. *Step Up: Building a Workforce for the Future. The Role of Education and Training in Wisconsin Works (W–2).* Madison: Wisconsin Department of Workforce Development, June 1998 [http://www.dwd.state.wi.us/desw2/Govw2etc.htm].

Huston, M. "Agencies Urge Lawmakers to Alter W-2." *Milwaukee Journal Sentinel,* Sept. 16, 1998, p. B1–B2.

Institute for Wisconsin's Future. *The W–2 Job Path: An Assessment of the Employment Trajectory of W–2 Participants in Milwaukee.* Milwaukee: Institute for Wisconsin's Future, 1998.

Knell, S. *Learn to Earn: Issues Raised by Welfare Reform for Adult Education, Training, and Work.* Washington, D.C.: National Institute for Literacy, 1998 [http://www.nifl.gov/activities/sknell.htm].

Krueger, L. "New York City Welfare Reform 1998: Job Centers Are Replacing Income Support Centers." Community Food Resource Center, New York, New York. Unpublished paper, September 1998.

National Governors' Association. *Summary of Selected Elements of State Plans for Temporary Assistance of Needy Families.* Washington, D.C.: Employment and Social Services Policy Division, National Governors' Association Center for Best Practices, 1997 [http://www.nga.org/CBP/Activities/WelfareReformHotTopics.asp#State].

National Governors' Association. *Strategies to Promote Education, Skill Development, and Career Advancement Opportunities for Low-Skilled Workers.* Washington, D.C.: Employment and Social Services Policy Division, National Governors' Association Center for Best Practices, 1998 [http://www.nga.org/Pubs/IssueBriefs/1998/980728Career.asp].

National Institute for Literacy. *Learning Disabilities and Welfare-to-Work: Part I.* Washington, D.C.: National Institute for Literacy, 1998.

Strawn, J. *Beyond Job Search or Basic Education: Rethinking the Role of Skills in Welfare Reform.* Washington, D.C.: Center for Law and Social Policy, 1998a.

Strawn, J. *Senate Amendment to Welfare LawAllows States to Train Hardest-to-Employ Adults, Help Others Find Better Jobs.* Washington, D.C.: Center for Law and Social Policy, 1998b.

Swarns, R. "Hispanic Mothers Lagging as Others Escape Welfare." *New York Times,* Sept. 15, 1998, pp. A1, A29.

U.S. Department of Labor. *About Welfare—Myths, Facts, Challenges and Solutions.* Washington, D.C.: U.S. Department of Labor, 1998 [http://www.doleta.gov/resources/myths.htm].

USWorkforce.org. *The Workforce Investment Act* [http://usworkforce.org.wialaw.txt], 1998.

Watson, K., and Gold, S. *The Other Side of Devolution: Shifting Relationships Between State and Local Governments.* Washington, D.C.: The Urban Institute, 1998 [http://newfederalism.urban.org/html/other.htm].

White, C., Ziegler, M., and Bingham, B. *Families First: Implications of Welfare Reform for Tennessee Adult Basic Education.* Knoxville: Center for Literacy Studies, University of Tennessee, 1998.

ELISABETH HAYES is professor of curriculum and instruction and faculty member in the Graduate Program in Continuing and Vocational Education at the University of Wisconsin-Madison.

2

The transformation of adult basic education programs resulting from welfare reform and workforce development goals raises serious philosophical and ethical questions that affect the funding, development, implementation, and evaluation of adult education programs.

Critical Issues and Dilemmas for Adult Literacy Programs Under Welfare Reform

Barbara Sparks

> Our organization is very disappointed that many welfare-to-work programs developed via welfare reform downplay the need and importance of adult basic education.
> —Adult basic education instructor, Nebraska

> The pressure for full-time employment makes education more unattainable at a time when, in my opinion, it is needed the most.
> —Adult basic education director, Nebraska

Because of its emphasis on Work First, the Welfare Reform Act of 1996 has placed increased pressure on adult basic education programs (ABE) to provide education and training that will help welfare recipients gain quick employment. Although states vary in their implementation of the Temporary Assistance for Needy Families (TANF) legislation based on their geography, economics, and politics, some basic underlying issues remain constant for adult educational programs. Issues arise out of a specific context and vary depending on one's perspective: thus there is a need to understand the current historical moment of economic and social upheaval; to understand the conservative mood of the country, which undergirds current societal change; to identify pressing concerns related to this context; and to consider how best to respond to the country's new social policies.

    The emphasis of TANF on quick employment brings to the forefront the contrast between two competing forms of adult basic education (ABE) practice. The struggle between ABE for purposes of social action and change and ABE for individual instrumental growth and economic development is dramatically played out within the arena of welfare reform. The unquestioning notion that there could be an opportunity for increased enrollment in ABE programs because of people's need for education to gain work is quickly problematized when ethical questions or concerns about the power of education for social control are raised. In other words, the role of ABE in welfare reform stands in stark contrast to the values and beliefs of many ABE practitioners.

This chapter looks at some of the critical issues and dilemmas confronting ABE practitioners interested in providing instruction for welfare recipients. The first section presents competing perspectives on cultural values, the economy, and patriarchy. From the issues raised within these perspectives, three sets of dilemmas emerge for ABE practitioners. Each is addressed in turn, concluding with a discussion of the implications of these dilemmas for ABE practice.

Competing Perspectives

Significant structural conditions, such as the globalization of production, the widening gap between the rich and the poor, the economic and social gains of women and people of color during the 1970s and 1980s, increased immigration (especially from Mexico), and the conservative ideology of family values at work in contemporary society provide the sociohistorical context for this round of reform measures and for the decisions responsible ABE practitioners will have to make in their wake. What is touted as a move to get welfare recipients, who are predominately women, off of public assistance and on a path toward self-sufficiency can be read very differently from different perspectives.

One liberal-to-moderate view holds that single mothers should work outside the home to earn their own way and contribute to the country's economic growth and development. Since women from traditional middle-class two-parent families have made their way into the labor force, it is expected that all women can and should do the same. Those who hold this view see no problem with requiring poor women to enter the labor market within a two-year time period, even though these women have very different educational experience and skill levels than those of the middle class. Despite increases in state spending, there is a lack of sufficient public child care, complicating matters further: poor women simply cannot make enough money to pay for private child care. In addition, the reform's work provisions permit full-time caregiving when there are two parents but forbid it when there is only one (Mink, 1998).

Progressive perspectives have broadened the issues beyond those of self-sufficiency to include issues of economic justice (see Sparks in Hayes and others, 1998). For example, in a fact sheet on workfare and nonprofits, Mimi

Abramovitz tells us that if "every new job in New York City were given to a welfare recipient (470,000 in 1996), it would take 21 years for all recipients to be absorbed into the economy" (Abramovitz, 1997, p. 2). In Wisconsin, not only are there not enough jobs for all welfare recipients, but the percentage of jobs available that are low-skill jobs would leave two out of three job seekers with no job: "There are 73 low-skill job seekers for every living-wage entry-level job in the state" (Institute for Wisconsin's Future, 1998b, p. 3). A similar scenario is predicted in many other communities, both rural and urban. The fact that there are not enough jobs counters the myth that any welfare recipient who wants a job can find one; additionally, the fact that family-supporting wages will be available for only a fraction of the five million welfare recipients who will be forced to leave the welfare rolls is obscured. Again, looking at Wisconsin, "only 4 percent of low skill jobs pay a living wage, $25,907 for a family of three" (Institute for Wisconsin's Future, 1998b, p. 3). In a report calculating the minimum cost of supporting a family in Nebraska, Patricia Funk (1998) states that we are likely to promote "working poverty" rather than economic self-sufficiency by believing the myth that low-skill jobs provide enough money for families to live on. Without family-supporting wages, it is impossible for recipients to move out of poverty and join the middle class.

Feminists contend that the sexual division of labor, whereby women are routinely tracked into certain positions, helps cement poor women's inferior position in the economy. Racism compounds this problem for women of color, subordinating them even further and reserving the lowest-paying jobs for them. Gwendolyn Mink, cochair of the Women's Committee of One Hundred, states that, especially for women of color, "wage work has been a mark of inequality: expected by the White society for whom they work; necessary because their male kin cannot find jobs or cannot earn family-supporting wages; and exploitative because their earnings keep them poor" (1998, p. 25). Another aspect of gender-based economic inequality in the United States is the fundamental division between paid labor in the public sector and unpaid labor in the home, or private sector (Hart, 1996), which demeans women's caregiving role and renders them dependent on men or the government. Some feminists hold that resilient patriarchal social constructs and gender relationships constitute even stronger variables than the economy for shaping social policy, through the perpetuation of a "family ethic" (Abramovitz, 1997) and the "patriarchal necessity" of control (Miller, 1990). But despite these barriers to women in society and the economy, the politics of welfare reform has legislated self-sufficiency as a means of achieving cultural and behavioral reform of welfare mothers.

TANF brings into question whether social policy should dictate that women work outside the home. Mandating that they do fosters the oppression of women by giving them minimal choice and by clinging to a "one-size-fits-all" mentality. Add to this the shortage of living-wage jobs, even in a boom economy, for all welfare recipients who must enter the labor force within the next two years. These contradictory conditions exist simultaneously, reinforcing the social and economic domination of women.

The competing and partial perspectives discussed thus far highlight some of the salient issues from which at least three sets of dilemmas emerge. These can be thought of as overlapping areas of concerns that adult literacy programs and practitioners must address. They include ideological dilemmas, which take into account underlying values, beliefs, and contradictions of social programs; educational dilemmas, which address program purposes and goals and the status of adult literacy in this country; and ethical dilemmas, which center on questions of dignity, respect, and accountability. These areas of concern are raised based on informal interviews and surveys with adult basic education administrators in the rural and urban Midwest (Sparks, 1998), structured and unstructured interviews with welfare recipients in rural and urban settings (Sparks, 1998; Sparks and MacDaniels, 1999), research studies of practice and policy related to adult education and welfare-to-work initiatives (Funk, 1998; Strawn, 1998; D'Amico, 1997; Barton and Jenkins, 1995; Institute for Wisconsin's Future, 1998a; Murphy and Johnson, 1998), and my participation in a June 1998 symposium looking at the impact of welfare reform on adult literacy, sponsored by the National Center for the Study of Adult Learning and Literacy and the National Institute for Literacy.

Ideological Dilemmas

The ideology of U.S. contemporary society is found in its values and beliefs about people (as individuals and as groups), people's interactions, relationships between individuals and their communities, beliefs about how daily life should proceed, the role of the state in social life, and the societal norms that are fostered. This ideology manifests in the form of consensual and, often, conflicting laws, procedures, strategic actions, and discourses. Ideological differences often arise over social policy, such as welfare reform and adult education policies. In the nineties, the ideological differences between the patriarchal, economically tied forces behind welfare reform and the socializing, mechanistic structures of adult education have come head to head.

The first paragraph of the preamble to the Personal Responsibility and Work Opportunity Reconciliation Act (PRWORA) of 1996 states that "Marriage is the foundation of a successful society." The act goes on to redefine the purpose of welfare, as follows (PL 104–193, Title I, section 101, 401 as cited in Mink, 1998):

1. To provide assistance to needy families so that children can be taken care of in their own homes or in the homes of relatives
2. To end dependence of needy parents on government benefits, by promoting job preparation, work, and marriage

3. To prevent and reduce out-of-wedlock pregnancies
4. To encourage the formation and maintenance of two-parent families.

Although the second stated purpose relates most directly to adult education, it must be viewed within the full context of the act to understand the TANF contract system and the lives of the recipients tied to the two-year time limit. The law's principal emphasis, promoting a "family ethic" (Abramovitz, 1997), is obscured by its focusing exclusively on job preparation and work. There is no mention of education, either to find work or to gain a credential. Job preparation conjures images of job search activities, job clubs, phone banks, resume writing, and interviewing—in other words, the model that has been used for many years by state and county employment offices. It assumes that what people need are incentives to find work. Under the TANF system, states are accountable for enrolling recipients in work or work-related activities, with strict definitions about what constitutes such activity. The mandates to increase both the number of recipients in work-related activities and the number of hours they must work pressures states to adopt a Work First emphasis.

There is not a single, unified ideology for ABE programs. Rather, the dual ideologies within adult education—one espousing individual development, the other calling for social involvement and action through education—create tension within the field. The adult education legislation in the Workforce Investment Act of 1998 espouses an individual-development philosophy, with an emphasis on the social roles of adults as workers, providers, and parents. It assumes literacy is required to obtain the knowledge and skills necessary for employment and self-sufficiency and to participate in one's children's educational development. Additionally, there is an implicit acknowledgment that a high school degree is needed to get a job. The act's underlying individualist assumptions are revealed by statements concerning individual inadequacies, the need to fill gaps in people's knowledge and skills, social and economic conformity, and standardization of programs. The fact that adult literacy will be regulated by the Labor Department more tightly links the agenda of education to the goal of supporting work.

The importance of the Equipped for the Future project (Stein, 1995) points to another force in the ideological struggle occurring in adult literacy programs—the values of adult learners. The National Institute for Literacy asked 1,500 adult education students to identify what adults want literacy programs to prepare them to do. To compete in the global economy and exercise their rights and fulfill their responsibilities as citizens, the respondents said, adults need

- Access to information, so they can orient themselves in the world
- The ability to voice their ideas and opinions, and confidence that they will be heard and taken into account

- The ability to take independent action to solve problems and make decisions in their multiple roles as adults
- "A bridge to the future"—learning *how to learn,* so they can keep up with the rapidly changing world

Undergirding this project is an individualist ideology, yet it highlights the broader interests of adults that go beyond education for work to include civic and cultural participation; continuous growth, development, and learning; social interaction; and decision making. These are integrated skills and processes that adults need in their families, in their communities, and as participants in the civic life of the nation.

Struggle over Ideologies. The competing ideologies between welfare reform and adult education, as well as those within the field of adult education itself, create dilemmas for practitioners that are not easily resolved. The emphasis on job preparation under welfare reform results in very different types of programs and services from what an emphasis on individual growth and the development of academic skills yields. However, the current firm capitalist grip on government has created a situation in which state authority over education has tightened. The link between the economy and education has been predominant for some time, as global capitalism has grown and demanded unskilled and skilled workers to fill particular sectors of the labor force; this is nothing new. Nevertheless, the ideological shift required of education under PRWORA will also continue to be contested, if not by educators themselves then by individuals seeking to achieve their own educational goals.

The differing ideologies also point to differing views of poor women. ABE acknowledges the dual (if not multiple) roles single mothers play in contemporary society, as parents and workers—both of which require literacy skills. By contrast, the welfare reform movement sees poor women as dependent, living off the government while others are "carrying their own weight." Yet, not all other mothers are required to work. Middle-class, two-parent families do not require their mothers to work; these mothers are given a choice—but they are contributing to the foundation of a successful society by being married.

Other dilemmas may surface as well, such as the struggle to reconcile one's personal values with the demands of an ABE position in the age of welfare reform. Can an ABE practitioner train poor women according to the tenets of Work First yet adhere to a set of personal values based on fairness, justice, women's rights, and personal choice? Do poor women have the right to the same things we want for ourselves, such as career choice, child-care options, and the freedom to move at one's own pace along life's path?

The fundamental issues of ideology frame the way life is lived in social contexts, how institutions are created and managed, how people are treated, and the value placed on social advancement. Ideology is the springboard for understanding the educational and ethical issues raised in the next two sections.

Educational Dilemmas

Educational dilemmas emerge inside ABE programs as administrators, teachers, and others attempt to make sense of their roles and their relationship to welfare reform measures. Questions about program design and evaluation, student assessment and progress, differing circumstances of adult learners, program accountability, and the status of adult literacy become problematic because of the underlying tensions between TANF legislation and ABE programs. Two issues will be examined here: the difference between TANF and ABE program goals and purposes and the current status of literacy programs in the United States.

Program Goals and Purposes. As discussed previously, ideological differences between TANF and ABE result in inherently different program purposes and goals. ABE programs are being asked to shift their formats to accommodate welfare reform requirements. This is a major source of conflict between welfare reform proponents and ABE practitioners (D'Amico, 1997), due not only to conflicting ideologies but also to the imbalance of power between economic and educational interests.

In an effort to reduce needy families' dependency on the government, the welfare reform movement has adopted a strategy of putting people to work at all costs—an approach known as Work First. There is a preoccupation on the part of corporations and the state with the "quick fix" of job searching, and the Work First approach supports the two-years-and-out mandate (Strawn, 1998). Although this works for some recipients, reports such as the follow-up study to the National Adult Literacy Survey (NALS) by Barton and Jenkins (1995) show that almost half of welfare recipients have very low skills and no high school diploma or GED. This quick fix will not help these individuals (mostly women) achieve self-sufficiency. Rather, it demoralizes them, because they cannot find adequate jobs at their skill level, or the jobs they do find are temporary or part-time (Weisberg, 1998). According to the Institute for Wisconsin's Future (1998b), the W–2 program (Wisconsin's welfare reform program, which relies on quick fix strategies) does not adequately address the gap between the education and skill levels required by employers and those possessed by the population of welfare recipients. D'Amico (1997) and others (Romero, 1994; Strawn, 1998) state that, historically, jobs programs with an emphasis on employment, such as the GAIN program in California and similar programs, do not lead to living-wage jobs either. Without an educational credential and adequate academic skills, even those who can find work will not be able to sustain employment or find higher-paying, more stable jobs. (According to Parrott [1998], individuals with a GED receive 19 to 29 percent higher quarterly earnings than do people without one.)

An adult literacy approach is interested in building the learner's academic skills, the lack of which is the most common barrier to finding and keeping work (Strawn, 1998). According to ABE practitioners, this approach seeks to prepare people for additional education or vocational training and to provide systematic education for workforce development (Sparks, 1998). The goals of ABE are thus broader and more inclusive than mere job preparation or quick fixes: this type of educational commitment is a longer-term strategy. The length of time it takes to develop academic skills is a consistent challenge for ABE practitioners, yet there is no shortcut for it. As new models are developed (Murphy and Johnson, 1998; Strawn, 1998; among others), what educational wisdom, teaching strategies, and curricular content will be forfeited to comply with the reform measures?

Many adult literacy programs offer activities that encourage people to engage in learning projects to solve local problems. For example, some offer auxiliary programs on topics such as health care, parenting, citizenship, community development, service learning, and economic literacy (Rivera, L., personal communication, June 19, 1998). Practitioners worry that women will not want to participate in these types of programs because such programs do not count toward fulfilling welfare contract requirements— welfare recipients are now driven by the Work First model and short-term training requirements.

Another substantial difference between welfare reform policies and ABE programs is in their divergent standards and guidelines for defining success, whether for students or for programs. Most ABE programs, from community-based programs to discrete skill–building programs, use guidelines that focus on learning and applying skills in everyday life. TANF, by contrast, focuses on the amount of time recipients put in at a training or educational site and on their subsequent accountability to caseworkers and their TANF contracts. TANF drops recipients in the middle of programs if they are not complying with attendance requirements, which obviously interferes with their learning. Who, then, defines success for these learners? What gets counted—learning and skill building, or attendance? Whose standards are used to move the learner forward? If TANF defines success strictly in terms of participation in education or training that fits the two-year limit—regardless of whether that training actually provides participants with adequate skills—where does that leave individuals who are left unprepared but must still find work that will support their families? In a similar vein, who defines what constitutes successful adult literacy programs if there is no agreement on what counts as student success? Programs that do not help recipients find employment are considered failures regardless of the skills participants come away with (Strawn, 1998).

Contemporary Status of Adult Literacy. Adult literacy programs have historically been underfunded and understaffed, many relying solely on volunteer tutors due to a shortage of funds to hire enough teachers. The same situation continues today; indeed, it is accelerating with the demands of TANF. Inadequate funding and understaffing have left some rural communities without literacy programs or with programs that are located too far away to serve the rural poor (Sparks, 1998). In some locations program sites are open fewer than the twenty hours a week that TANF requires. The problem of limited services is compounded if there is no nighttime child care for evening classes. For many rural recipients, transportation is another problem. In an informal interview, an administrator from one rural service area in the Midwest related that the small ABE center she is in charge of must provide services for fifteen counties (Sparks, 1998). To serve the welfare recipients being referred from these counties, more volunteers have been recruited to provide individual tutoring at locations closer to where the women live; there are no funds to hire teachers for the TANF clients.

Urban ABE programs face different circumstances from those faced by rural programs, but the effects on recipients are similar. For many large urban programs, welfare recipients are confronted with waiting lists or caseworker delays and cannot get into programs. In smaller urban programs, particularly community-based programs, lack of computer equipment, competition for funding, and lack of state support make it difficult to serve welfare recipients at all. Many midsized cities do not have adequate public transportation, making it impossible for many women to get to programs on time after they see their children off to school (Sparks, 1998).

Relationships between federal- and state-level health and human services (HHS) and ABE programs indicate little interagency collaboration, communication, or team strategies for remedying underfunded programs or moving people to self-sufficiency (Sparks, 1998; Imel, 1998). There has been little communication beyond participant referrals and reporting of attendance or outcome data (D'Amico, 1997). Similarly, HHS agencies have not tapped the accumulated knowledge of ABE practitioners about adult development, learning, and literacy, nor do they use practitioners' case conferences and recommendations regarding individual learners, except in unusual situations. Connie White (1998) presented a study on the impact of welfare on adult literacy at a symposium cosponsored by the National Center for the Study of Adult Learning and Literacy and the National Institute for Literacy, which revealed the concerns of ABE instructors in the South. According to her report, the low level of involvement by ABE administrators and practitioners in developing policy and procedures that directly affect ABE programs has created a sense of isolation. This, coupled with less-than-adequate funding to provide services to welfare recipients, has some ABE people worried. Armed with few resources and only fragmented knowledge about local TANF statutes, ABE practitioners are caught in a similarly invisible position as are the women on welfare, where lived experiences and knowledge is not valued and solutions are directed downward from the capitalist state. It should not be surprising, then, that most ABE programs get no money from HHS agencies and have no contracts with them to provide services.

Differing program purposes and goals for welfare recipient learners, plus the low status accorded ABE programs in this sociohistorical moment, handicap ABE practitioners. Will the program changes required by TANF serve the educational interests of welfare recipients or the interests of the government? Will ABE programs be able to afford to provide special services for welfare recipients while maintaining their traditional programs? How can ABE programs serve welfare clients without adequate funding from and collaboration with the state, particularly when they are held accountable by the state? ABE practitioners need to use political strategies and negotiation skills to advocate the educational principles that are grounded in their work. The logic of academic development for long-term learning, growth, and prosperity will support the capitalist economy and move people toward economic justice, not just off welfare.

Ethical Dilemmas

Ethical ABE practice considers power relationships and the pragmatic necessity of negotiating between the interests of divergent groups, including welfare recipients, government, and the public. As ABE practitioners move back and forth between these interests, conflicts can be identified in the implementation of TANF. This section examines the role of women's voices in implementation, the role of ABE programs in monitoring recipient behavior, and the status of instructors.

Are there yardsticks by which ethical judgments can be made? Cervero and Wilson (1994) call for a model of adult education that is substantially democratic and that asks such questions as "Who actually represents the learner?" "When are learners involved?" and "In what judgments do they participate?" We must carefully consider the intended consequences—and try to imagine the unintended consequences—of the choices that our society and our ABE programs make. Who will stand with the recipient learners—the single mothers who must make it to self-sufficiency regardless of the level of their vocational and academic skills and of whether or not they are receiving the promised and legislated supports of child care, food stamps, transportation, and health care assistance, which can mean the difference between success and failure? At what strategic points in the process, if any, do welfare recipients have the opportunity to voice their choice from among various educational or training options?

Women's Voices. While ABE programs try to deal with the mandates imposed on them by welfare reform, other ethical issues emerge. Despite what we know about the need for advanced education and training to secure and hold living-wage jobs (Parrott, 1998; Institute for Wisconsin's Future, 1998a), welfare recipients' interests and voices have been left out of the equation. Yet, women and women's needs will be the principal stakeholders and concerns in the reformulation of the welfare state (Fraser, 1989). Education is being cut as an option for many recipients, insofar as they are being discouraged from pursuing education or barred from enrolling in programs that can make a difference in their lives. We need to ask who is allowed to participate in adult education, under what conditions, and for what reasons.

Mink (1998) and others contend that individual rights to vocational free-dom and education and to train for chosen work as suggested by the Thir-teenth Amendment, freedom from coerced labor, are being violated: "The TANF work requirements limit vocational education to one year; limits the number of adult recipients who may be enrolled in vocational education, withdraws encouragement of higher education, does not provide basic edu-cation unless that education is specifically related to employment and does not adequately fund job training" (Mink, 1998, p. 111).

A qualitative study of over forty welfare recipients in the Midwest (Sparks, 1999) verified that recipients experience educational stratification. The study documented the lack of choice in educational and training pro-grams for welfare recipients and the practice of tracking them into short-term job training rather than two- or four-year degree programs (which are the surest way out of poverty). Some recipients are told by caseworkers that they are too old to enter training programs; those who have some work skills are considered "employable" even if their skills will not get them a job that will support their families. Some must hold down two part-time jobs to continue higher education programs, which do not count toward work requirements. Who will listen to these voices? When will they be taken into account? Whose interests are being served by "ending welfare as we know it," as President Clinton has promised to do?

Role of Literacy Programs. A politics of control undergirds welfare reform (Mink, 1998). TANF's tight control on how education and training are defined establishes a chain of command whereby ABE programs must trans-form their format, content, and delivery to coincide with the time limits of welfare mandates, regardless of the time it takes for low-skill learners to progress. Likewise, the required restructuring of two-year vocational programs determines the skill level of trainees and the subsequent job responsibilities and positions they will be prepared to take on. As training is "dumbed down," learners are denied access to jobs requiring higher skill levels.

Adult education programs are caught in the middle, between the man-dates of TANF and their clients' needs. TANF calls on ABE programs to monitor and control the behavior of welfare recipients through strict report-ing of their participation and to enforce sanctions administered by case-workers to noncompliant recipients who do not put enough classroom hours into their educational studies. The power of the welfare policy and its determination to eliminate needy families' dependency on the government is seen at the federal level, where legislation funding adult basic education is contained in the Workforce Investment Act, administered by the Secre-tary of Labor.

D'Amico (1997) poses another ethical dilemma when she asks practi-tioners to consider what it means to implement policies that see job place-ment as a necessary outcome of education. To what degree will ABE programs become more complicit in endorsing "learning for work" (a tech-nical approach) at the expense of "learning for life"? Some programs are looking for ways to adapt adult education to accommodate short-term training segments and more limited goals rather than the goal of obtaining a GED; considerable effort at the federal and local levels is expended on designing academic programs with an employment focus. What values of ABE practice are compromised? Perhaps to soften the sting, some ABE practitioners have absolved themselves of responsibility for the social-control function of the schooling they provide: "I do not really see it as an ethical issue from the ABE side. We are not the ones deciding their [recipients'] futures—as much as the HHS workers" (Sparks, 1998, p. 15). How well we fool ourselves.

Status of Instructors. Finally, considering the weight of the federal mandate to put people to work, it may seem surprising to find that little, if any, federal money is being put into hiring or developing professional instructors with the necessary background to teach adult learners. Rather, while welfare recipients are being forced to find full-time employment that will take them and their families off welfare, adult literacy programs are using a disproportionate number of volunteer and part-time ABE instructors, who receive no benefits (White, 1998).

As "hard to place" recipients make their way through the new welfare regulations, more and more learning disabled adults will languish in inadequate programs. What level of professional expertise will part-time teachers and volunteers, many of whom have little or no educational training, be able to provide? To understand this contradiction, one simply needs to reflect on the chronic underfunding of ABE and the public's stereotyped view of individuals with low literacy skills: "The perception is that undereducated adults are a social problem that has cost this nation billions of dollars in lost income and taxes in addition to the money spent for welfare programs and prisons" (Sparks and Peterson, forthcoming). The insufficient number of professionally prepared instructors available for ABE sends a clear message that literacy students do not deserve them.

In summary, ethical dilemmas abound in ABE programs, in the lives and education of women on welfare, and in the relationship between ABE programs and government mandates. The democratic practice model of Cervero and Wilson (1994) instructs practitioners to take an ethically pragmatic approach, an approach that ultimately leads one to make decisions based on justice and care.

Implications

I have raised these critical questions and dilemmas concerning responsible ABE practice to lead up to what I consider the number-one question ABE practitioners and programs must decide: whether or not to participate in the welfare reform movement as it is currently structured. If the decision is made to proceed, then the next question must be "In what way do we want to be a part of that system?" ABE programs and practitioners must decide if they will serve welfare recipients or the state, how they can maintain program and professional integrity, and how they can advocate for essential changes for recipient learners and for democratic programs. Further, questions about the effect of this new social policy on local ABE program development, implementation, funding, evaluation, and policy need to addressed. Some programs may decide that providing workforce education does not fit their philosophy and purpose. In other words, "the only way to plan responsibly is to act politically" (Cervero and Wilson, 1994, p. 117). Achieving pragmatism with vision requires that "all people who are affected should be involved in the deliberation of what is important about the programs. . . . Planners must carry out this vision within a context of power that either threatens or supports this vision" (p. 154).

The report *Equipped for the Future* (Stein, 1995), in which adults articulated their educational needs and desires for the purposes of social action and intervention, provides another model of practice ABE programs might choose to emulate. Further, should critical literacy (a literacy that attempts to uncover the dynamics between social relations and societal structures and institutions) play a role in the welfare reform movement, and what might programs designed to promote it look like? Advocating equal citizenship rights and responsibilities for all classes and races and both genders will require women to voice their ideas and opinions and demand to be heard. This will take courage; however, to do less puts all women at risk.

References

Abramovitz, M. *Workfare and the Non-Profits: Myths and Realities.* New York: National Association of Social Workers, 1997.

Barton, P., and Jenkins, L. *Literacy and Dependency: The Literacy Skills of Welfare Recipients in the United States.* Princeton, N.J.: Educational Testing Service, 1995.

Cervero, R., and Wilson, A. *Planning Responsibility for Adult Education: A Guide to Negotiating Power and Interests.* San Francisco: Jossey-Bass, 1994.

D'Amico, D. *Adult Education and Welfare to Work Initiatives: A Review of Research, Practice, and Policy.* Teaneck, N.J.: National Institute for Literacy, 1997.

Fraser, N. *Unruly Practices: Power, Discourse, and Gender in Contemporary Social Theory.* Minneapolis: University of Minnesota Press, 1989.

Funk, P. *Economic Self-sufficiency: The Minimum Cost of Family Support in Nebraska, 1997.* Lincoln: Nebraska Appleseed Center for Law in the Public Interest, 1998.

Hart, M. "Literacy and Motherwork." In J. P. Hautecoeur (ed.), *Basic Education and Work.* Toronto: Culture Concepts, 1996.

Hayes, E., and others. "Talking Across the Table: A Dialogue on Women, Welfare, and Adult Education." *39th Annual Adult Education Research Conference Proceedings.* San Antonio: University of the Incarnate Word and Texas A&M University, 1998.

Imel, S. *Work Force Education or Literacy Development: Which Road Should Adult Education Take?* ERIC Digest, no. 193. Washington, D.C.: ERIC Clearinghouse on Adult, Career, and Vocational Education, 1998.

Institute for Wisconsin's Future. *The W–2 Job Path: An Assessment of the Employment Trajectory of W–2 Participants in Milwaukee.* Milwaukee: Institute for Wisconsin's Future, 1998a.

Institute for Wisconsin's Future. *Transitions to W–2: The First Six Months of Welfare Replacement.* Milwaukee: Institute for Wisconsin's Future, 1998b.

Miller, D. *Women and Social Welfare: A Feminist Analysis.* New York: Praeger, 1990.

Mink, G. *Welfare's End.* Ithaca, N.Y.: Cornell University Press, 1998.

Murphy, G., and Johnson, A. *What Works: Integrating Basic Skills Training into Welfare-to-Work.* Washington, D.C.: National Institute for Literacy, 1998.

Parrott, S. *Welfare Recipients Who Find Jobs: What Do We Know About Their Employment and Earnings?* Washington, D.C.: Center on Budget and Policy Priorities, 1998 [http://www.chpp.org/11–16/98wel.htm].

Romero, C. *JTPA Programs and Adult Women on Welfare: Using Training to Raise AFDC Recipients Above Poverty.* Washington, D.C.: National Commission for Employment Policy, 1994.

Sparks, B. "The Impact of Welfare Reform on Adult Literacy Programs Survey." Unpublished report, Sept. 1998.

Sparks, B. "Poor Women's Education Under Welfare Reform." *Adult Education Research Conference Proceedings.* Northern Illinois University, 1999.

Sparks, B., and MacDaniels, C. "Women in Community Making Meaning: A Participatory Approach to Understanding Poor Women's Subjectivity." Manuscript submitted, 1999.

Stein, S. *Equipped for the Future: A Customer-Driven Vision for Adult Literacy and Lifelong Learning.* Teaneck, N.J.: National Institute for Literacy, 1995.

Strawn, J. *Beyond Job Search or Basic Education: Rethinking the Role of Skills in Welfare Reform.* Washington, D.C.: Center for Law and Social Policy, 1998.

Weisberg, R. *Ending Welfare as We Know It* [film]. Public Policy Productions. Available from Film Makers Library, New York, New York, 1998 (1999 is the year released; 1998 is the year produced).

White, C. "Families First: Implications of Welfare Reform for Tennessee Adult Basic Education." Paper presented at NCSALL/NIFL conference, Rutgers University, June 1998.

BARBARA SPARKS is assistant professor, Department of Vocational and Adult Education, University of Nebraska-Lincoln.

3

This chapter discusses empirical research on former welfare recipients and programs designed to serve them in the welfare-to-work transition.

Research on Adult Literacy Education in the Welfare-to-Work Transition

James C. Fisher

Changes in federal and state law and policy that have resulted in dramatic shifts in the nature and delivery of public assistance programs have also affected the nature and delivery of adult basic education (ABE) programs. The traditional role of ABE programs—to improve students' literacy, broaden their functioning, and move them toward achieving an educational credential or other goal—has been deemphasized in favor of finding them employment not subsidized by the government. Many official documents, including legislation and official policy statement, fail to acknowledge that basic education is an element in the transition from welfare to employment.

The purpose of this chapter is to examine the empirical research that has analyzed the role of adult literacy programs in helping recipients make the transition from welfare to work successfully. The discussion is organized around characteristics of the welfare recipient population, program characteristics, program goals and emphases, and program outcomes.

The selection of research presented here is limited by several factors: some research is national in scope and seems to have little relationship to factors integral to local programs; other research is strictly local, addressing specific local program characteristics, and has limited applicability to the larger scene. Such research is limited by unidentified variables implicit in the context, such as the health of the local economy, which affect programs dealing with employment. It is also limited by a short-term time frame: the programs and approaches being measured have existed only a few years, and during that time many have undergone significant modifications. Few of the studies on this topic have addressed threats to internal validity, such as the impact of events external to the study, or external validity, such as the use of nonexperimental methodologies. Furthermore, most of the findings being interpreted within the context of TANF legislation were from studies conducted on the JOBS program. Because of basic differences in these two legislative approaches, questions may legitimately arise concerning the applicability of research from one program generation to another.

Participant Characteristics

This section presents findings from studies describing the literacy proficiency of the population at large as well as that of the welfare-to-work population. It also discusses the impact of literacy proficiency and other characteristics of this segment of the population as they relate to employability.

Literacy Skills of the Population at Large. Data describing literacy proficiency are presented to provide a point of comparison between the population at large and former welfare recipients. The National Literacy Act of 1991 suggests the following definition for *literacy:* "an individual's ability to read, write, and speak in English and compute and solve problems at a level of proficiency necessary to function on the job and in society, to achieve one's goals and to develop one's knowledge and potential" (National Center for Education Statistics, 1996, p. 2). Building from this definition, the National Adult Literacy Survey (NALS) divided literacy into three categories (National Center for Education Statistics, 1996):

1. *Prose literacy* is the ability to locate and use information from texts such as newspapers, stories, poems, and so on.
2. *Document literacy* is the ability to interpret and use information in charts, tables, graphs, maps, indexes, and so on.
3. *Quantitative literacy* is the ability to perform arithmetic operations using information embedded in both prose texts and document materials.

Each of these three types of literacy can be measured at five levels of proficiency. According to the National Center for Education Statistics (1996, p. 7), the large percentage of persons demonstrating proficiency at the lowest level for each category (21 percent for prose literacy, 23 percent for document literacy, and 22 percent for quantitative literacy) may be explained by participation of immigrants unfamiliar with the English language, persons who terminated their education before completing high school, older adults, and those with physical, mental, or health conditions that inhibited their full participation in work, school, or home activities.

Literacy Skills of the Former AFDC Population. Several studies describe the literacy skills of that segment of the population that until recently received welfare and currently are involved in welfare-to-work transition programs. Isolating data from welfare recipients from those of the population at large in the National Adult Literacy Survey (Barton and Jenkins, 1995) reveals that

1. From one-third to almost one-half of all welfare recipients performed at the lowest literacy level on a five-level scale, and approximately one-third performed at the second-lowest level. In the welfare recipient population, the proportion of those performing at the lowest and second-lowest level ranged from 60 to 80 percent, compared with 48 percent for the population at large. Between one-quarter and one-third of welfare recipients performed at level three or higher; just 7 percent performed at levels four and five.
2. The average literacy level of welfare recipients is below that of unskilled laborers and assemblers in the general population.
3. The performance differences found between males and females, whites and blacks, and whites and Hispanics in the population at large are smaller in the welfare recipient population, indicating that lack of literacy proficiency is spread across all demographic groups within this population.
4. Employed former welfare recipients with higher literacy levels earn higher wages than do their less literate counterparts; the higher the literacy level, the more weeks former welfare recipients worked in the preceding year.

Demographic Profile of AFDC Recipients. Data reported by the Urban Institute in 1996 profiled the welfare population still further:

- Over 90 percent of welfare families are single mothers.
- About 19 percent of welfare cases consist of children only.
- Most welfare mothers are in their twenties or thirties.
- Welfare mothers are 37 percent white, 36 percent African American, 20 percent Hispanic, and 6 percent from other groups.
- About 40 percent have not received a high school credential.
- The average number of children in a welfare family is fewer than two.
- Over two-thirds of women on welfare had some recent work experience before applying for public assistance.
- Although the mean duration of benefits is 6.5 years per family, about 42 percent of families receive benefits for fewer than two years.

In addition, according to Demetra Smith Nightingale, estimates of the number of welfare recipients with learning disabilities range from 25 to 40 percent of the welfare population (cited in Cohen, 1998).

A study of an innovative approach to improving the well-being of low-income adults and children in Milwaukee identified three major barriers to acquiring full-time employment—having limited work experience, having very young children, and lacking an educational credential (Bos and others, 1999).

According to the National Institute for Literacy, welfare recipients are characterized by low literacy skills: young adults on welfare read, on average, at the sixth-grade level. The relationship between the educational level of welfare recipients and the length of time they receive benefits is strong: nearly two-thirds of those with a high school diploma or GED leave the welfare rolls and become self-sufficient within two years, but over 60 percent of those who spend more than five years on welfare had less than a high school education when they began receiving benefits. Welfare recipients with low literacy skills work an average of eleven weeks per year, compared with twenty-nine weeks for those with stronger literacy skills (National Institute for Literacy, 1998). According to the New York State Education Department (1997, p. 1), possession of a high school or GED credential or job training nearly doubles the probability of a welfare recipient's working and staying employed. The studies just cited describe characteristics of AFDC recipients, but the link between educational level and employment is most clearly demonstrated by the experience of those now attempting the transition from welfare to work. Large numbers of former welfare recipients are being placed in unsubsidized employment, leaving those with less education and less work experience among the unemployed. It is this population of hard-to-place individuals for whom education and training programs are being developed. But according to Elliott, Spangler, and Yorkievitz (1998, p. 17), it is still easier for a person with limited skills and credentials to find a job than it is for such a person to keep a job and advance in it.

Program Characteristics

Discussions of research on the characteristics of ABE programs that support the welfare-to-work transition occurs against the backdrop of traditional adult literacy programs. Findings from both research and practice in traditional adult literacy education speak of difficulty attracting and retaining students in general, and poor attendance and high dropout rates of AFDC recipients in particular (Cohen and others, 1995). Although research findings attest to the strong link between education and economic success, researchers have had difficulty connecting traditional adult education program outcomes with job success. In *Equipped for the Future*, Stein (1997, p. 4) shows that

- Students in traditional federally funded adult education programs spend insufficient time in the programs to make progress (median retention rates range from less than sixty hours per learner to thirty-five hours for native English speakers with the lowest skill levels).
- Traditional programs feature school-based subject matter and a remedial approach rather than methods and content responsive to what adults want and need.
- These programs receive about $258 per student to provide literacy instruction, and 80 percent of the teachers are part-time and lack the means to systematically document outcomes.

As a result, traditional adult education programs fail to demonstrate effectiveness in achieving labor market success.

According to the National Center for Research in Vocational Education (NCRVE), most federal job training programs fail to connect classroom instruction with work-based learning or to combine academic and vocational education. Programs funded by the Adult Education Act are "freestanding, unconnected to either vocational skills training, work-based instruction, or higher-level programs" (National Center for Research on Vocational Education, 1995, p. 1). Furthermore, these remedial programs are described as using "outdated modes of didactic instruction, often because they are driven by the GED," fostering insubstantial learning on the job, and being "unconnected to remedial academic or vocation skills training and to any further training opportunities" (p. 1).

Based on its evaluation of eighty-four educational programs developed under TANF, the National Institute for Literacy identified common denominators of eight successful programs developed to support the welfare-to-work transition (Murphy and Johnson, 1998, p. 13). The following factors were examined or considered in assessing these programs (pp. 1, 50):

- The number of recipients who achieved either a job or a successful outcome related to preparing themselves for the workplace
- The quality of the educational services offered, as determined by (a) assessment of students, (b) basic skills services offered that are relevant to participants' needs and related to the skills needed for work, (c) use of case management to coordinate services, and (d) degree of integration with other components of the welfare-to-work program
- The selection process for participants, including the extent to which more difficult to place recipients were included
- Records on enrollment, student achievements, and costs, which together reveal the costs associated with participant progress and outcomes
- Private sector involvement in program planning, implementation, and placement of participants in jobs

The common characteristics of the eight exemplary programs are as follows (pp. 13–16):

- *Focus on employment-related goals.* "In the most successful programs, the goal of employment is manifest from the outset and permeates the instructional program" (p. 14). Although the work requirements may differ depending on the local job market, successful programs are organized around work-related requirements.
- *Hands-on experience.* The utility and relevance of the skills taught in the classroom are demonstrated in participants' internships, job shadowing experiences, or actual employment. In some programs, both classroom and worksite learning are incorporated into the program.
- *Collaboration with welfare agencies and other community organizations.* Successful programs see beyond the educational needs of their participants

and connect them with agencies that deal with other needs, such as child care, health, housing, violence and abuse, transportation, and so on.

- *Early intervention and personal attention in addressing problems.* Exemplary programs tend to assign a particular staff member responsibility for coordinating the many aspects of support required to ensure a participant's retention and employment. The effectiveness of this effort depends on prompt intervention in problems that affect the participant's progress toward obtaining employment.
- *Commitment to continuous staff development.* Successful programs emphasize staff training and sponsor opportunities for staff members to meet regularly to share experiences and learn from one another.

These characteristics of successful educational programs in the TANF era describe a practice in which the workplace context provides both the goal of employment and the setting into which the learning activities are integrated. Community agencies provide necessary support services.

These recommendations for practice stand in contrast to findings by Purcell-Gates of the Harvard Graduate School of Education, who examined traditional literacy programs nationwide on the basis of two axes: life-contextualized practice versus life-decontextualized practice, and dialogic practice versus monologic practice. Life-contextualized programs create their literacy program from materials that are relevant to students' lives, such as newspapers; life-decontextualized programs focus on identified skills and use workbooks and materials supplied by publishers rather than materials generated by students. In dialogic practice students are involved in all aspects of the program, including boards and committees responsible for establishing class rules; in monologic programs teachers determine or select all content, activities, and materials. In her study of 271 programs in forty-two states, Purcell-Gates found that the majority (73 percent) of programs were life-decontextualized and monologic. However, most programs were clustered in the center of each of the two continua, midway between life-contextualized and life-decontextualized and between dialogic and monologic. Few programs were located at the extremes of either continua. The study concluded that "this reflects teachers' intentions to address two competing approaches: the need for skills and the need for students to determine their own course of study" (Purcell-Gates, 1997, p. 2). Purcell-Gates's work illumines the sharp contrast between traditional literacy programs, in which students' life context counts for little, and the programs developed in support of TANF, in which employment provides the only significant context and the only function of learning is to support employment.

The welfare-to-work transition has created a major shift in the practice of basic skills education for welfare recipients, from ABE as a discrete, standalone educational process to its integration into a larger scheme that includes social services and classroom and workplace learning partnerships with the clear purpose of achieving employment for the participants.

In an earlier study of single welfare mothers engaged in a successful pre-employment educational program, Irene Baird (1995) concluded that the wages from employment were insufficient to offset the reduction in benefits, leading her to argue that any approach that focuses on education as the single solution to reducing welfare dependence is inadequate. Others have joined this argument, suggesting that education and training are inadequate solutions to major structural problems of the economy that result in pockets of unemployment and underemployment (D'Amico, 1996).

Program Goals and Emphases

Of all of the changes that have resulted from the welfare-to-work transition, none is more dramatic than the change in the delivery of literacy education, from long-term to short-term and from the general to the specific (for a more detailed discussion of this shift, see Chapter One).

Holcomb, Pavetti, Ratcliffe, and Reidinger (1998) list several ways in which states have customized education and training to fit the priorities of workforce development in the TANF era, with its emphasis on quick entry of welfare recipients into the workforce: "(1) permitting recipients to engage in education and training only after completing a job search that has proven unsuccessful, (2) permitting participation in education and/or training only when it is coupled with more work-oriented activities (i.e., job search or unpaid work experience) and (3) providing more education and training activities on a more flexible, open-entry basis so that participants do not have to wait for long periods of time before starting a work-related activity" (p. 26). Further, they describe a shift away from longer-term basic education and toward short-term education. On the basis of a study of Work First and work-oriented programs in six states, they judge the states to be in the "early stages of exploring how education and training could be restructured to complement a Work First approach, as opposed to simply [being] deemphasized" (p. 27).

To accommodate these contextual changes, delivery systems that coordinate public assistance intake processes with job search services, work activities, education and training, and other services have been established to integrate application for assistance, support services such as food stamps and child care, and preparation for work under the larger heading of "workforce development." One consequence has been the development of integrated case management systems, "[to] infuse a greater focus on employment and self-sufficiency into the eligibility process" (p. 59); another has been the development of centers providing broad job placement and employment assistance for all.

Still another consequence, perhaps unintended, has been the curtailment of student involvement in and multisource government support of stand-alone literacy agencies. Reuys (1996) describes the impact of career centers on a literacy education provider in Somerville, Massachusetts. The provider's income fell from $228,000 to $84,000, requiring staff layoffs and sharply reducing the number of students recruited and enrolled in its program.

The Manpower Demonstration Research Corporation (MDRC), under contract with the U.S. Department of Health and Human Services, the U.S. Department of Education, and other state and local funders, has conducted major research addressing the contextual shift from literacy education to workforce development for welfare recipients. This research captured the essence of the contextual shift from "human capital development" (HCD), which emphasizes longer-term, skill-building education and training activities, to the approach characterized as "labor force attachment" (LFA), which emphasizes rapid job entry. The major difference between the two approaches is the amount of education and training provided prior to job placement. The intent of both approaches is to help welfare recipients increase their earning power and their ability to stay off public assistance for the long term (Hamilton and others, 1977).

For MDRC's study, AFDC recipients at three sites were randomly assigned to an LFA group, an HCD group, or a control group, which neither had access to the program nor was subject to program requirements. The LFA group emphasized "taking the first job that came along," and the HCD group emphasized investing in education and training and being more selective. Both programs were mandatory for participants; nonparticipation was greeted with sanctions that resulted in grant reductions. Further, the HCD programs cost about twice as much as the LFA programs, although most of these costs were born by nonwelfare agencies (Hamilton and others, p. 4). Following are the results for each group.

LFA Program Results:

- Increased participation in job-search. "LFA sample members were seven times more likely to engage in job search than their control group counterparts" (p. 13).
- Increases in employment earnings relative to what would have happened in the absence of a mandatory welfare-to-work program. "The LFA programs increased earnings by more than $1,000 per average sample member [over control group members] in each of the three sites" (p. 16).
- Savings in AFDC expenditures relative to what would have happened in the absence of a mandatory welfare-to-work program. The LFA programs reduced welfare expenditures by $368, to $1338, representing a savings of 7 to 18 percent relative to the welfare payments control group members received (p. 17).
- Reduction in joblessness. One of five welfare recipients who would not have worked in an unsubsidized job during the period did so, and the proportion of individuals on AFDC at the end of the two-year follow-up period decreased from 7 to 11 percent. Nevertheless, between 50 and 68 percent were receiving welfare at the end of the period, and between 38 and 50 percent were both receiving AFDC benefits and were unemployed (p. 18).

HCD Program Results:
- Increased participation in adult basic education, from two to six times the proportion of those in the control group (p. 19). At two of the sites, the percentage of participants obtaining a high school diploma or GED increased by ten percentage points (p. 4).
- Small first-year earnings increases, which grew during the second year at two sites. At the third site, which included only individuals who did not complete high school, a moderate first-year earnings impact decreased in the second year. At the other sites, employment and earnings were smaller for those lacking high school credentials (p. 22). In fact, those without high school credentials in the HCD groups were subject to welfare reductions not offset by earnings gains (p. 28). The earnings increases overall were smaller than those produced by participants in the LFA group (p. 5).
- Reduced welfare expenditures by $333, to $1,134, depending on the site. These reductions represented savings of between 6 and 11 percent, relative to the welfare payments that control group members received (p. 24).

The researchers concluded that "both the LFA and HCD programs decreased the proportion of individuals who remained continuously on the welfare rolls throughout the two-year follow-up period" (p. 5). Sanctions designed to increase participation by reducing welfare benefits failed to achieve that result (p. 5). The researchers also concluded that "a time frame of two years . . . is not long enough to observe the full effects of these two approaches" (p. 32).

Given the shift in context to the Work First approach of TANF, many recommendations for practice fail to take into account the diversity of the welfare-to-work population, neglecting in particular those persons whose lack of basic skills—compounded by a limited education, personal and social problems, limited work experience, and minority status—will likely result in significant difficulty placing them in unsubsidized employment or other work-related activities without special programs.

In an evaluation of the effectiveness of California's Greater Avenues for Independence (GAIN) program (Friedlander and Martinson, 1996), GED certificates and improved achievement test scores were obtainable outcomes for AFDC recipients with relatively high pretest scores. However, researchers concluded that those with lower pretest scores would require substantially more effective programs and those with the lowest literacy levels would require programs that take entirely new approaches to the organization and delivery of literacy education. In addition to low basic skills, key characteristics of those considered harder to serve include some combination of the following: little or no previous work experience, mental health problems, substance abuse, domestic violence, child behavior problems, and legal problems (Holcomb, Pavetti, Ratcliffe, and Reidinger, 1998, p. 27). A study of Milwaukee County, Wisconsin, single-parent AFDC families revealed that 75 percent of those who left AFDC in the first quarter of the study had been employed one year earlier; these individuals were older and better educated and had fewer children than those who remained on welfare. Those who returned within three months had fewer than twelve years of schooling and no work history during the preceding fifteen-month period (Pawasarat, 1998).

According to Holcomb and colleagues, providers that place greater emphasis on this hard-to-serve population

- Used case managers "to work more intensively to identify and resolve barriers for those who do not find jobs" (p. 28)
- Required welfare-to-work recipients to attend an "addictions awareness" session and be screened for potential chemical dependency
- Offered mental health counseling to recipients and help for case managers experiencing difficulty working with a particular client
- Required treatment or counseling for those with abuse or mental health problems as a condition for receiving benefits. Time spent in these activities counted toward the participation requirement.

Although research findings have not adequately addressed the longer-term impact of literacy on employment, significant studies are examining the outcomes of particular contextual approaches of ABE on the welfare-to-work transition. These findings also call attention to the extreme lack of basic skills, educational attainment, and work experience, plus the personal and social problems that place members of this subpopulation at risk.

Program Outcomes

Any discussion of outcomes of welfare-to-work programs must begin with the caveat that information generated by the states and federal government has generally not been adequate to support decision making for a nationwide program. Methodological inconsistencies and simple lack of data notwithstanding, emerging findings from evaluations of state programs as well as studies by the federal government suggest that some outcomes may be identified from welfare-to-work programs that have been established in the states. For example:

- The number of people on welfare nationwide fell from 14.1 million in January 1993 to 8.9 million in March 1998, a 37 percent decline. Twenty-seven percent of this decline occurred since the reforms were signed into law in August 1996 (Pear, 1998).
- The national evaluation by MDRC of state-run employment and training programs shows that the best way to move welfare recipients from dependency on welfare to employment is to place them in jobs as quickly as possible. Individuals in LFA programs experienced increased rates of employment and earnings and significantly decreased their dependence on

public assistance and food stamps. The employment rate for participants in programs that stressed education and training was less than one-third the rate achieved by the LFA approach. Earnings were lower than for those who had received AFDC (National Center for Policy Analysis, 1998, p. 8).

• Programs had limited success in reducing long periods of unemployment or AFDC recidivism: although 40 to 45 percent of all AFDC recipients studied left the rolls within two years, up to 75 percent of those who left returned to welfare within the next seven years (National Center for Policy Analysis, 1998, p. 11).

• Gains in earnings by former welfare recipients in many programs have exceeded program costs, with the result that reductions in AFDC have exceeded program costs, leaving a net budget surplus.

• Success in placing former welfare recipients in unsubsidized employment may not result in long-term job security, advancement, or better-paying jobs for them in the future. Data from employers describe a mismatch between their requirements and the skills of the former welfare recipients they have hired. A study of Wisconsin employers revealed that expectations for unskilled jobs included reading and math skills, computer skills, the ability to handle machinery and equipment, and the ability to read measuring instruments, skills frequently unavailable among the welfare population (Institute for Wisconsin's Future, 1998, p. 18). Similarly, Lafer (cited in D'Amico, 1996) describes entry-level positions for former welfare recipients that are unconnected to the organization's career ladder, limiting their potential for advancement within that organization.

The dramatic success of LFA approaches in reducing welfare costs during a period of labor shortages, combined with the absence of convincing data to connect long-term education and training programs with employment goals, has refocused the discussion of the role of basic education in job preparation. The limited time frame of the studies, the absence of longer-term employment histories, and the positive state of the national economy during the welfare-to-work transition render the current picture incomplete at best. Questions that press for answers concern the ultimate fate of those at risk of chronic unemployment and the relationship between basic skills and long-term employment success.

Summary and Conclusion

Changes in law and policy have resulted in dramatic shifts in the nature and delivery of public assistance programs and have affected adult basic education programs. According to the National Institute for Literacy, welfare recipients are characterized by low educational skills: data indicate that possession of a high school or GED credential or job training dramatically increases their likelihood of finding employment. However, a principal outcome of welfare reform is that job searching, unpaid work experience, and subsidized jobs play key roles in preparing welfare recipients for employment, and education and job training have been deemphasized so that welfare recipients can be required to secure immediate jobs or work activities. Findings also call attention to the heterogeneity of the welfare recipient population, particularly with respect to the educational, personal, and social problems that place members of this subpopulation at risk for chronic unemployment.

References

Baird, I. C. "Learning to Earn 'The Right Way': Single Welfare Mothers in Mandated Education Programs." Unpublished doctoral dissertation, Pennsylvania State University, 1995.

Barton, P. E., and Jenkins, L. *Literacy and Dependency: The Literacy Skills of Welfare Recipients in the United States. Policy Information Report.* Princeton, N.J.: Educational Testing Service, 1995. (ED 385 775)

Bos, H., and others. *Executive Summary. New Hope for People with Low Incomes: Two-Year Results of a Program to Reduce Poverty and Reform Welfare.* New York: Manpower Demonstration Research Corporation, 1999.

Cohen, E., and others. *Literacy and Welfare Reform: Are We Making the Connection?* National Center on Adult Literacy Technical Report no. TR94–16. Philadelphia: University of Pennsylvania, 1995. (ED 378 366)

Cohen, M. "Education and Training Under Welfare Reform." *Welfare Information Network Issue Notes,* 1998, 2 (2), 3.

D'Amico, D. "The Emperor's New Jobs: Welfare Reform, Unemployment and Education Policy." *Urban Anthropology,* 1996, 25 (2), 165–194.

Elliott, M., Spangler, D., and Yorkievitz, K. *What's Next After Work First.* Field Report Series. Philadelphia: Public/Private Ventures, 1998.

Friedlander, D., and Martinson, K. "Effects of Mandatory Basic Education for Adult AFDC Recipients." *Educational Evaluation and Policy Analysis,* 1996, 18 (4), 327–337.

Hamilton, G., and others. *Executive Summary. The National Evaluation of Welfare-to-Work Strategies. Evaluating Two Welfare-to-Work Program Approaches: Two-Year Findings on the Labor Force Attachment and Human Capital Development Programs in Three Sites.* New York: Manpower Demonstration Research Corporation, 1997 [http://www.mdrc.org/].

Holcomb, P., Pavetti, L., Ratcliffe, C., and Reidinger, S. *Building an Employment-Focused Welfare System: Work First and Other Work-Oriented Strategies in Five States.* Washington, D.C.: U.S. Department of Health and Human Services, 1998 [http://www.urban.org/welfare/workfirs.htm].

Institute for Wisconsin's Future. *The W–2 Job Path: An Assessment of the Employment Trajectory of W–2 Participants in Milwaukee.* Milwaukee: Institute for Wisconsin's Future, 1998.

Murphy, G., and Johnson, A. *What Works: Integrating Basic Skills Training into Welfare-to-Work.* Washington, D.C.: National Institute for Literacy, 1998 [http://www.nifl.gov/whatworks.htm].

National Center for Education Statistics. *1992 National Adult Literacy Survey.* Washington, D.C.: U.S. Department of Education, 1996 [http://nces.ed.gov/nadlits/naal92/].

National Center for Policy Analysis. *Welfare to Work.* Dallas, TX: National Center for Policy Analysis, 1998 [http://www.public-policy.org/~ncpa/pi/welfare/wel25.html].

National Center for Research on Vocational Education. *Legislative Principles for Career-Related Education and Training: What Research Supports. Principle 9.* Berkeley, Calif.: National Center for Research on Vocational Education, 1995 [http://ncrve.berkeley.edu/Principles/p9.html].

National Institute for Literacy. *Fact Sheet: Literacy and Welfare.* Washington, D.C.: National Institute for Literacy, 1998 [http://www.nifl.gov/newworld/WELFARE.HTM].

New York State Education Department. *Welfare Reform: Roles That Education Can Play* 1997, [http://www.nysed.gov/workforce/wfroles.html].

Pawasarat, J. *Employment and Earnings of Milwaukee County Single Parent AFDC Families: Establishing Benchmarks for Measuring Employment Outcomes Under W–2.* Milwaukee: Milwaukee Employment and Training Institute, University of Wisconsin-Milwaukee, 1998 [http://www.uwm.edu/Dept/ETI/afdscearn.htm].

Pear, R. "More Welfare Recipients Going to Work, Study Finds," *New York Times,* June 19, 1998.

Purcell-Gates, V. *U.S. Adult Literacy Program Practice: A Typology Across Dimensions of Life-Contextualized/Decontextualized and Dialogic/Monologic.* Cambridge, Mass.: National Center for the Study of Adult Learning and Literacy, Harvard Graduate School of Education, 1997 [http://hugse1.harvard.edu/~ncsall/report2.HTM].

Reuys, S. *The Economies of SCALE: Exploring the Impact of Career Centers on ABE Programs,* 1996. (ED 401 403)

Stein, S. G. *Equipped for the Future: A Reform Agenda for Adult Literacy and Lifelong Learning.* Washington, D.C.: National Institute for Literacy, 1997.

The Urban Institute. "A General Profile of the Welfare Population." Washington, D.C.: The Urban Institute, 1996 [http://wtw.doleta.gov/ohrw2w/recruit/urban.htm].

JAMES C. FISHER is associate professor of adult and continuing education at the University of Wisconsin-Milwaukee.

4

This chapter defines the parameters and limitations of the academic model of adult literacy program development and presents a framework that includes three other approaches: situated context and cognition, literacy integrated with soft skills, and literacy integrated with occupational skills.

Continuum of Literacy Program Models: Alternative Approaches for Low-Literate Welfare Recipients

Larry G. Martin

When federal and state initiatives on welfare reform and workforce development were first introduced, the ramifications of the changes caught many literacy practitioners by surprise. They expected change but anticipated they could survive with minor adjustments. At that time most adult literacy programs pursued learner development via traditional academic curricula. Such curricula allowed low-literate welfare recipients long-term opportunities to gain a GED, high school diploma, or competency diploma. However, as the reform measures have been implemented, they have not only affected the extent to which low-literate recipients receive government support to attend literacy classes, they have caused differential effects in the programs themselves. One of their most visible effects is in patterns of enrollment in literacy programs. Examples of these effects include the following:

- Declining enrollments (see Chapter One) due to the number of clients placed in mandatory jobs
- Changes in the types of students likely to enroll, since learners with lower literacy skills are mandated to attend literacy programs, but those with higher skills are placed directly into jobs
- Changes in students' motivations for enrolling, due to an increase in mandatory versus voluntary participation
- Changes in the amount of time, such as the number of hours per week, students have available for literacy study

NEW DIRECTIONS FOR ADULT AND CONTINUING EDUCATION, no. 83, Fall 1999   © Jossey-Bass Publishers

- Changes in the time of day (that is, day versus evening hours) students are available to participate
- The potential loss of federal and state funding for literacy programs that lack a Work First orientation

These reforms target only welfare recipients, who make up just one segment of the population from which literacy programs draw their students (other literacy students include workers, family literacy students, incarcerated low literates, and so on). However, the nature and extent of the reforms are destined to usher in a new era of literacy programming as literacy practitioners contemplate the role of literacy education in helping welfare recipients obtain employment and advance in the workforce. This chapter presents a framework of alternative literacy education approaches that could help practitioners expand their offerings to meet a wider variety of needs among current and former welfare recipients. The following topics are discussed: employment tiers and the literacy needs of recipients, continuum of literacy programs, and synthesis of employment tiers with continuum of programs.

Employment Tiers and the Literacy Needs of Recipients

Federal and state legislative initiatives categorize recipients in accordance with their employment placement potential, which roughly correlates with the level of literacy education needs among current and former welfare recipients. Assuming that participants who lack prior work experience can benefit significantly from an experiential exposure to the world of work, the Personal Responsibility and Work Opportunity Reconciliation Act (PRWORA) of 1996 identified both unpaid work experience and government-subsidized employment as acceptable means to meet the new federal work participation requirements for welfare recipients with either little work experience or low basic skills. However, as the reform measures have been implemented, a continuum of both former and current welfare recipients has emerged: unsubsidized employed workers, subsidized employed workers, subsidized unemployed recipients, and unsubsidized unemployed (often homeless) individuals.

Unsubsidized Employed Workers. These workers are considered "leavers" from the welfare rolls—that is, they no longer receive cash payments from the government. Brauner and Loprest (1999) analyzed eleven studies of leavers conducted by ten states. Only studies that clearly described their methodology and reported survey response rates of 50 percent or higher were included in Brauner and Loprest's analysis. They found that over half of the leavers worked thirty hours or more per week in jobs, such as restaurant, clerical, or retail sales and services. In general, they did not earn enough to raise their income far above the poverty level. Brauner and Loprest observed, for example, that in 1997 the poverty threshold for a three-person family with two dependent children was $12,931, the equivalent of full-time (thirty-five hours per week), full-year employment paying $7.39 per hour. However, the average earnings for leavers was estimated to be between $10,000 to $12,000, less than the poverty level for a family of three. Also, over half of leavers' families were still covered by Medicaid, and some leavers continued to receive food stamps. Leavers also relied on various nongovernmental sources of income, such as family and friends. Although leavers will take time to make the adjustment to a more independent lifestyle, many of them can still benefit from literacy programs. For example, in Wisconsin, 77.6 percent of leavers did not complete high school (Wisconsin Works Education and Training Committee, 1998). Also, some states, such as Wisconsin, even provide state support for such individuals to return to literacy classes six to nine months after they have left the welfare program. The state will pay for 50 percent of the child-care costs associated with returning to school.

Subsidized Employed Workers. These individuals work for private employers that pay subsidized employees with funds diverted from welfare programs. In the five states studied by Holcomb, Pavetti, Ratcliffe, and Reidinger (1998)—Massachusetts, Virginia, Oregon, Indiana, and Wisconsin—subsidized employment was a seldom-used option. However, Oregon has enjoyed considerable employer, legislative, and staff support for its "JOBS Plus" subsidized employment program. In the other states, use of subsidized employment was usually limited to a few select areas where an arrangement had been worked out among a few employers. One major barrier to the development of such programs is the difficulty of making an appropriate fit between the job needs of employers and the needs, interests, abilities, and skill levels of welfare recipients. Also, if recipients have skills sufficient for subsidized employment, they are generally able to find unsubsidized employment. Therefore these individuals would not likely be placed in mandatory literacy training programs, and they appear to share the same literacy needs as unsubsidized employed workers.

Subsidized Unemployed Recipients. These individuals represent two categories of recipients: those placed in unpaid community service jobs (CSJs) and transitional recipients.

Recipients Placed in CSJs. The unpaid work experiences for these individuals are often structured so that participants work for public and non-profit employers in exchange for welfare benefits. There is no direct financial exchange of work for benefits, however. Holcomb, Pavetti, Ratcliffe, and Reidinger (1998) found that in all five of the states they studied, telling recipients that they would be placed in an unpaid work-experience position served as a negative incentive to their seeking unsubsidized employment. Although such programs are used sparingly because of the administrative and operational challenges associated with them (especially during periods of strong economic growth and plentiful entry-level jobs), Holcomb, Pavetti, Ratcliffe, and Reidinger (1998) observed that community service providers found their experience with such workers mutually beneficial, and they were willing to help participants succeed in their assignments. However, recipients generally cut their assignments short and rarely remained in a position beyond one or two months. If such efforts fail to result in unsubsidized employment, then participants would be strong candidates for mandatory enrollment in literacy programs to assist their efforts.

Transitional Recipients. These individuals are considered harder to serve than those placed in CSJs. They do not qualify for unsubsidized employment without other support services, such as mental health services, substance abuse counseling, or vocational rehabilitation services. These individuals have particularly severe personal or family problems, such as substance abuse, health problems, depression, or a child with a chronic medical condition or serious disability. Therefore, more intensive strategies are required to address their needs. Holcomb, Pavetti, Ratcliffe, and Reidinger (1998) identified several steps taken by states to address this population. In addition to their other challenging characteristics, these individuals may also have mild to severe learning disabilities and thereby require specialized literacy education to address their learning needs.

Unsubsidized Unemployed Individuals. This category includes former recipients who either stopped receiving benefits voluntarily or were cut off as a result of sanctioning. Although none of the studies reviewed indicated how many individuals and families left welfare because of sanctioning, Brauner and Loprest (1999) found that sanctioned leavers had a lower employment rate compared with other leavers. Their employment rate ranged from 39 percent in Tennessee to 53 percent in Michigan and Iowa. Also, in a survey of 62 homeless families residing in a homeless shelter in Milwaukee, Wisconsin, 32 percent indicated that they had been sanctioned at some time since the introduction of welfare reform (Center for Self-Sufficiency, 1999). However, eleven of the twenty sanctioned respondents indicated that their current spell of homelessness was unrelated to the sanctioning.

Given the range of low-literate welfare recipients and former recipients identified above, traditional academic literacy programs will be hard-pressed to continue to meet their learning needs in the normal way. Successful pre-employment and worksite-based educational programs must be designed to work in concert with other social services, and they should include short-term programs that target the specific needs of these learners. Therefore, adult literacy providers must become more creative in their efforts to deliver educational programs that meet the learning needs of current and former low-literate welfare recipients.

Continuum of Literacy Programs

The challenge now is for literacy practitioners to develop a continuum of programs that provide an appropriate mix of literacy instruction, with varying degrees of context and skills (that is, broad or narrow; see Table 4.1),

Table 4.1. Mix of Literacy Programs Targeting Welfare Recipients

	Broad Context	Narrow Context
Broad Skills	*Academic Programs:* for example, basic skills programs, GED programs, competency-based programs, and so on	*Integrated Literacy with Occupational Skills Training:* for example, welding programs, machine operation training, Certified Nursing Assistant programs, and so on
Narrow Skills	*Literacy Integrated with Soft Skills and Life Skills Training:* for example, job readiness programs, family literacy programs, and so on	*Situated Context and Cognition:* for example, workplace programs

that can help current and former recipients both acquire and maintain employment. In addition to academic programs, three other approaches are currently being considered or implemented in efforts to improve literacy instruction, knowledge retention, and students' motivation: situated context and cognition, literacy integrated with soft skills, and literacy integrated with occupational skills (Cohen and others, 1995). This transition from the more traditional, "academic" approach represents a significant change not only in the philosophical orientation of literacy instruction but also in the entire process of designing, implementing, and evaluating literacy programs. This section discusses four types of programs that represent the mix of program alternatives available to literacy practitioners.

Academic Approach. The academic approach is the dominant form of adult literacy education. It focuses on the development of a broad base of academic knowledge and skills—such as the ability to read, the ability to write, and the ability to perform arithmetic operations—that are generalizable to a variety of contexts. It places a premium on "symbol manipulation," by which the learner is encouraged to master symbolic rules of various kinds (such as phonics), and mathematical formulas (Resnick, 1987). Based on the general curricula of high school, the instructional objectives, course materials, and class instruction of academic literacy programs are organized around the identification, manipulation, and mastery of laws; symbols, such as letters, words, numbers, formulas, and others; and well-defined problems that are abstractions taken from contextual situations. In addition, academic programs also value the learner's ability to think independently—that is, without the aid of physical and cognitive tools such as notes, calculators, and so on (Resnick, 1987). Therefore, welfare recipients placed in academic programs are taught symbol manipulation and independent thinking skills, with a focus on coding and decoding of abstract concepts (for example, solving word problems in preparation for the GED test).

The planning of academic programs is often conducted by literacy administrators in conjunction with literacy instructors and guided by the curricula of K–12 schools (Mezirow, 1996). According to the academic model, students learn best in classroom situations, using the tools of whole-group discussion, teacher-prepared individual and small-group practice exercises, workbook exercises, preplanned goals and objectives, and computer programs (Dirkx and Prenger, 1994). The programs are offered in a wide variety of settings, including high schools, community colleges, community centers, homes, and others. Instructors are usually current or former K–12 schoolteachers employed to deliver the literacy program on a part-time basis. The time commitment for students ranges from one week to over three years. At the completion of the program, students receive a certificate, such as a GED, a high school diploma, or another credential.

However, there is mounting evidence that academic programs may be inappropriate for those welfare recipients who have the lowest levels of literacy skills. In a study conducted prior to the welfare reform initiatives, Friedlander and Martinson (1996) found that the impact of attending academic literacy programs on welfare recipients was concentrated among those members of the sample who possessed higher initial literacy levels. The findings suggest that welfare recipients with lower literacy skills should be enrolled in alternative literacy programs, whereas those with higher skills are strong candidates for traditional academic literacy programming.

Situated Context and Cognition. The situated context and cognition approach is composed of an array of curricular approaches ranging from context-based programs to situated-cognition programs. The literature on workplace literacy abounds with examples and models of context-based programs that do not seek to help learners generalize beyond the specific context in which the knowledge they convey is taught. (See Chapter Five for a more detailed discussion of these programs.) Therefore, in the interest of expanding the theoretical options available to practitioners, this section discusses situated-cognition programs. Although no models or examples of these types of programs were found in the adult education literature, theoretically they provide a systematic way to help learners progress from familiar, context-specific knowledge and thinking (such as for a particular job or workplace) to more abstract, generalized knowledge and thinking consistent with the goals of the academic approach.

The situated-cognition approach has gained increasing attention in the K–12 literature as scholars have observed differences in how out-of-school learners, that is, everyday people and practitioners, and school students reason when they are presented with complex, ill-defined problems. The studies analyzed by Cobb and Bowers (1999) found that different forms of reasoning tend to arise in the context of different practices that involve the use of situation-specific tools and are organized around different overall motives. For example, when presented with a "reading" problem, a school student would tend to view the problem of learning to read as an end in itself. However, a worker would view reading as an important job skill that is critical to economic survival.

These scholars have observed that the academic approach to teaching and learning artificially separates what is learned from how it is learned and used. They argue that the activity by which knowledge is developed and deployed is not separable from or ancillary to learning and cognition. Rather, the situations in which learning occurs coproduce knowledge through activity (Brown, Collins, and Duguid, 1989). Learning is thereby viewed as an activity that is situated with regard to an individual's position in the world of social affairs in nonschool settings (Cobb and Bowers, 1999).

Brown, Collins, and Duguid (1989) identified two assumptions that are central to understanding situated knowledge and learning. The first pertains to both learning and tools. Learning how to use tools involves far more than can be accounted for in any set of explicit rules. The occasions and conditions for use arise directly out of the context of activities of each community that uses the tool, framed by the way the members of that community see the world. For example, a pair of scissors are indispensable for both barbers and seamstresses, yet each of these communities has its own rules for the correct use of scissors and their role in their work process. For novices in each community, learning and acting are therefore indistinct. Learning is a continuous, lifelong process and results from acting in situations. In this way, people who use tools build an increasingly rich implicit understanding of the world and of the tools themselves. The second involves learning and enculturation. Enculturation occurs when a person learns to speak, read, and write, for example, or becomes an employee in a specific organization. When given the chance to observe and practice, in a particular context, the behavior of members of a culture, people quickly learn the relevant jargon, imitate the behavior, and gradually start to act in accordance with the culture's norms, which can be extremely complex.

Four arguments are advanced in the literature that suggest education for welfare recipients should be situated in context-specific environments. First, there is a significant difference between "authentic activity"—that is, the ordinary practices of a given organizational or group culture—and school activity (Brown, Collins, and Duguid, 1989). The meaning and purpose of domain-specific activities are socially constructed through negotiations among present and past members of a community; therefore, activities that are coherent, meaningful, and purposeful to the community's members are authentic. School activity, such as classroom tasks, occur in a school culture, and success in this context often has little bearing on performance elsewhere. Therefore, such activity is inauthentic beyond the classroom and thus does not constitute fully productive learning experiences for individuals who do not have prior mental models of specific work environments.

Second, knowledge is "constructed" and does not transfer between tasks. Much of what a student learns is specific to the situation in which the learning occurs. Too often there is a mismatch between typical school (or academic) learning situations and "real-world" situations, such as the workplace, where learners are expected to display their knowledge (Anderson,

Reder, and Simon, 1996). For example, the lack of transfer of abstract knowledge taught in isolation from the context in which it will be used suggests that students might perform well in academic literacy classes but then struggle with written and spoken English in the workplace. Therefore, to be truly functional in a real-world context, learners must develop situation-specific forms of competence. In addition, learners taught via situated cognition would be encouraged to constantly test their knowledge against what they observe (Palincsar, 1989).

Third, learning is inherently a social, shared phenomenon (Resnick, 1987) that occurs in complex social situations, such as a workplace or family. This perspective recognizes that in out-of-school situations, most learning occurs through the use of knowledge tools (calculators, templates, procedural rules, and such) and knowledge sources, such as people who are experienced with the particular context. Therefore, literacy learners should be allowed to use the knowledge tools and sources found in typical (or targeted) work environments, and they should be required to display their skills in complex workplace situations. In addition, literacy students learn more efficiently when they use context knowledge and context-specific knowledge tools and sources to develop their literacy skills. In this way, literacy education is made more meaningful for them; this approach elicits greater participation and commitment from learners who need to see the relevance of their learning activities (Keeley, 1991).

Fourth, action is situationally grounded; the potentialities for action cannot be fully prescribed independent of the specific situation (Resnick, 1987). For example, preparation of an individual for a position as a nurse's aid cannot be complete with only an abstract discussion of the job context. The individual also needs to be exposed to the language and organizational culture of the employment setting; the roles and functions of the people, such as patients, nurses, and supervisors, with whom he or she will interact; and the job-related terms and situations with which he or she will contend on a daily basis as a nurse's aid.

A primary method of teaching via the situated-cognition approach is via a *cognitive apprenticeship* (Brown, Collins, and Duguid, 1989). This method supports learning in a contextual situation by enabling students to acquire, develop, and use cognitive tools in authentic contextual activity. It suggests situated modeling, coaching, and fading, whereby teachers or coaches promote learning by

1. Making explicit their tacit knowledge or modeling their strategies for students with an authentic activity.
2. Support students' attempts at performing the task, with the help of other students in the class.
3. Empower students to continue independently, by "fading." (See Brown, Collins, and Duguid, 1989, for further details on this method.)

Another important feature of cognitive apprenticeship is its emphasis on collaborative learning. This process seeks to enculturate learners through social interaction and the circulation of narratives through the conversations of groups of practitioners (Brown, Collins, and Duguid, 1989). It is characterized by students engaging in collective (group) problem solving; displaying, reflecting on, and discussing the multiple roles required for carrying out any cognitive task; confronting and discussing ineffective strategies and misconceptions; and practicing collaborative work skills.

Situated-cognition programs theoretically hold great promise as an alternative to the traditional academic approach. Short-term, career-focused job training can be provided via such programs for subsidized or unsubsidized, employed or unemployed recipients. Literacy providers can work directly with employers to develop on-site training opportunities.

Integrated Programs. Critics of the situated-cognition approach (Resnick, 1987; Anderson, Reder, and Simon, 1996) argue that situation-specific learning alone is very limiting. When familiar aspects of a task change in certain ways, they say, individuals educated by this approach may experience considerable difficulty or fail entirely. They suggest that the extent to which learning should be bound to a particular situational context depends on the kind of knowledge being acquired. In some cases knowledge can be bound to a specific context by the nature of instruction—for example, a process demonstration of word processing skills. In other cases, the extent of contextualization depends on the way the material is studied, such as hands-on problem solving (Resnick, 1987). Therefore, critics of the situated-cognition approach argue for an integrated model that embraces elements of both the traditional academic model and the situated-cognition approach. In the context of literacy programming, such an integrated model would seek to help learners develop a narrow base of skills (for example, job search skills) that are generalizable to a broad contextual base, or to develop a broad base of skills (for example, traditional academic skills) that will be applicable to a specific context, such as a particular job. Integrated programs attempt to integrate basic skills (academic) preparation with functionally meaningful content. The following arguments suggest that this approach can be viable for the preparation of low-literate welfare recipients.

First, the amount of knowledge transfer that occurs and the degree to which that transfer is positive depends on the learning experiences to which the learner is exposed and the relationship of the material that is originally learned to the transfer material (Anderson, Reder, and Simon, 1996). Therefore, learners can be taught workplace-specific skills (such as word processing or other computer skills) in classroom contexts, and those skills will transfer to a variety of employment settings so long as the content of the instruction is highly related to the requirements of the context in which those skills will be applied. In this view, representativeness and degree of practice are major determinants of transfer from one task to another and from one context to another.

Second, learning transfer varies directly with the number of symbolic (abstract) components that are shared in specific situations (Anderson, Reder, and Simon, 1996). The amount of transfer depends on where attention is directed either during the learning program or at the point of transfer. These observations suggest that, in preparing welfare recipients for success in the workplace, training on the cues that signal the relevance of a job-related skill should probably receive more emphasis in instruction than it typically receives in purely academic programs. A strategy of abstract instruction combined with concrete examples can be a powerful instructional method (Anderson, Reder, and Simon, 1996). This method is especially important when the knowledge gained from literacy programs must be applied to a wide variety of frequently unpredictable future tasks.

Third, observing that fewer cognitive resources are required for the actual performance of tasks than for learning them and that learning increases when large tasks are separated into smaller elements, supporters of the integrated approach argue that it is better to train people to perform independent parts of a task separately (Anderson, Reder, and Simon, 1996). Therefore, some of the skills required for context-specific jobs should be separated from the larger task requirements and taught in a classroom setting (Anderson, Reder, and Simon, 1996).

Two types of integrated programs are now being developed and implemented to assist current and former recipients: integrated literacy–occupational skills programs and integrated literacy–soft skills training.

Integrated Literacy–Occupational Skills Programs. Typically located in job centers, community agencies, and literacy centers, integrated literacy–occupational skills programs attempt to closely simulate the targeted job setting and integrate basic skills education with job skills training. Occupations are targeted that have a demonstrated lack of workers, and only twelve to twenty clients are allowed to participate in each program. The programs range from several days to twenty weeks in duration. They are typically designed by administrators in negotiated arrangements with potential employers, social services representatives and other payers, curriculum planners, and other stakeholders.

Murphy and Johnson (1998) assembled a panel of specialists in welfare, adult education, and employment and training and asked them to evaluate eighty-four programs that had submitted detailed information about their work. The panel selected eight programs that were exemplary. The Brooklyn Child Care Provider Program was one of the programs selected. This was a five-month literacy-based vocational training program through which graduates qualified for positions as assistants in child-care centers or to become self-employed family child-care providers. The program was structured so that basic skills instruction was highly contextualized with the child-care setting and integrated with a child-care curriculum; that is, literacy specialists teamed with early childhood specialists to design and implement the curriculum. Students alternated weekly between the classroom and internship worksites. This allowed students to apply skills and knowledge learned in the classroom in a hands-on learning environment on a continual basis. The program did not employ a formal reading or skills test as a condition of participation. However, all applicants were screened for employment in the child-care field; they had to pass clearances for child abuse, criminal convictions, and tuberculosis. The program utilized project-based instruction to implement the curriculum; that is, each topic was learned through completion of a project. For example, classroom instruction in nutrition and cost considerations in menu planning for child care concluded with the preparation of a two-week menu plan by each student. Discussion groups on topics related to activities in the worksite were held one morning per week so that students could learn from one another.

The planning and implementation of the program required collaboration among several agencies: the New York City Department of Employment; the Department of Health and Housing, to determine whether a participant's home was suitable for family day care; and both child protective services and the criminal justice system. At the completion of the program, participants received certificates from the New York City Department of Health authorizing them to operate their own family day-care centers, although many first gained expertise as employees in larger centers. Funded by the New York State Education Department, the program cost $4,711 per job placement, and it helped 88 percent of its sixty participants get jobs. Also, 10 percent earned their GEDs.

Integrated Literacy–Soft Skills Training. These programs tend to focus on a narrow set of social and organizational skills that can be applied to a much broader context. The literacy skills required to perform the targeted activities and functions can be taught conterminously with the training efforts designed to help participants acquire and develop the required skills. Programs have been developed (or they are being considered for development) on several important topics. For example, the Wisconsin Works Education and Training Committee (1998) recommended several types of training:

1. Training in job-seeking skills, to assist with the creation, preparation, development, and updating of resumes, the completion of job applications, and the development of networking skills
2. Job survival and retention training, to help participants understand the rules and expectations of employers, the qualities employers desire in an employee, the importance of punctuality, the ability to follow directions, the meaning of teamwork in the workplace, and so on
3. Life skills training, to allow parents to participate more fully in the workforce by helping them understand and accept their parental responsibilities, strengthen their parenting skills, manage their family

budget, manage their anger, develop their interpersonal skills, improve their problem-solving and decision-making skills, improve their time management skills, and so on

4. Motivational training, to get participants to overcome poor self-image by helping them identify their employment-related strengths and set long-term and short-term life and employment goals, creating an environment of encouragement and support, and providing mentoring experiences

Murphy and Johnson (1998) also identified the Canton City (Ohio) Schools' Even Start Program as an exemplar of the integrated approach. This program focused on teaching academic skills in context to fulfil participants' roles as parents, workers, and citizens as identified by *Equipped for the Future* (Stein, 1997). The program originated from a partnership between a local school district and a county department of human services. It served over one hundred families annually, at a cost of $1,914 per family. The structure of the program required thirty hours of class and work experiences per week. Both activities took place at participants' children's elementary schools. To qualify for participation, participants must have lacked a high school diploma and been a parent of at least one child under eight years of age. When they entered the program, 96 percent of the students received public assistance, and 51 percent read below the sixth-grade level. The curriculum was organized around *Equipped for the Future*'s generative skills. These skills are durable over time, in the face of changes in technology, work processes, and societal demands. They are transferable across the three primary adult roles: parent and family member, citizen and community member, and worker. The four generative skills areas are communication skills, interpersonal skills, decision-making skills, and lifelong learning. Students developed "individual career plans," in which they identified their skills and interests and appropriate career options. These plans included information on the local labor market, wages, education and training requirements for various jobs, and employer-specific information. Participants also developed and pursued short-term and long-term goals, including completing training requirements, organizing child-care and transportation, and securing an initial job. Students documented their achievements in a "career passport"—a portfolio used in job interviews.

The program collaborated with a wide variety of other agencies: local college students helped in classrooms, along with an America Reads VISTA worker; a local medical center provided health screenings and an eight-week job shadowing experience. Community business partners provided incentives, awards, and job shadowing opportunities; the Title I program provided child-parent learning activities; and the county department of human services assisted with the recruitment of families and funded career assessment activities and child care for children under age three. The program was funded from a variety of sources: an Even Start grant (57 percent), federal

ABE funds (29 percent), a federal 353 special demonstration grant (5 percent), and a National Center for Family Literacy grant (9 percent). At the completion of the program, 8 percent of families left public assistance, 21 percent of families secured a job for the first time (or got a better job), and 29 percent of parents passed either the GED or the official GED practice test.

Synthesis of Employment Tiers with Continuum of Programs. In this new era of literacy programming, adult literacy professionals are presented with an unprecedented opportunity to experiment with a number of different approaches to literacy instruction. Undoubtedly, some programs are more responsive to the needs of welfare recipients, whereas other programs are more appropriate for other learners. Table 4.2 provides an organizing framework for determining when narrower or broader contexts are required and when attention to narrower or broader skills are optimal for effective, efficient learning among the five types of recipient and former recipient learners.

Although the literature is inconclusive regarding the most effective matches between curricular approaches and types of current and former welfare recipients, it strongly suggested that academic programs tend to be successful with students who have experienced previous academic success. Given that other research has demonstrated a strong correlation between high academic achievement and employment, it is apparent that these programs could provide a significant means for both subsidized and unsubsidized employed workers to complete a secondary diploma or certification program. Such a credential could provide opportunities for both postsecondary education and career development. Also, some recipients in other tiers may also be close to finishing high school or may possess other characteristics to suggest they should also pursue academic programs. This option should remain open to such individuals. Additionally, the situated-cognition

Table 4.2. Employment Tiers and Learners Matched with Program Types

Employment Tiers and Types of Learners	Academic	Situated Cognition	Integrated Soft-Skills	Integrated Occupational Skills
Unsubsidized Employed	Y	Y	?	?
Subsidized Employed	Y	Y	?	Y
Subsidized Unemployed (CSJs)	?	?	Y	Y
Subsidized Unemployed (Transitional)	?	?	Y	Y
Unsubsidized Unemployed (Homeless)	?	?	Y	Y

Y = Yes. Should be a good match between the majority of learners and type of program.

? = Questionable. May not be a good fit between most learners and type of program.

programs are untested with adult literacy students, but given their emphasis on context, they may be most appropriate either for learners within employment settings or CSJs.

This program format also suggests that academic programs will be inappropriate (as currently designed and implemented) to serve the short-term literacy and employment needs of those current and former recipients with lower literacy skills. These learners will require different (more innovative) approaches to literacy instruction. Both situated-cognition and integrated programs seem to be appropriate for such learners, given their low literacy skills and their low level of previous work experience. Therefore, such programs could offer acceptable options for CSJs, transitional learners, and homeless learners.

Conclusion

A literacy provider system that promotes a continuum of programmatic options for current and former welfare recipients is optimal. In such a system, academic programs can help learners obtain credentials in order to pursue postsecondary opportunities and certify their knowledge attainment. Integrated programs can use the expertise of both literacy specialists and occupational and related skills specialists to design short-term learning experiences that teach literacy skills applicable both to job-related tasks and to the development of broad-based soft skills. Once students are either employed or engaged in employment-related training, literacy practitioners can use the situated-cognition approach to provide them with narrow, job-related, context-specific instruction regarding their employment responsibilities, teamwork, workplace norms, and so on.

References

Anderson, J. R., Reder, L. M., and Simon, H. A. "Situative Versus Cognitive Perspectives: Form Versus Substance." *Educational Researcher,* 1996, *26* (1), 18–21.

Brauner, S., and Loprest, P. "Where Are They Now? What States' Studies of People Who Left Welfare Tell Us." *New Federalism Issues and Options for States* (The Urban Institute), April 1999, *series A* (32), 1–10.

Brown, J. S., Collins, A., and Duguid, P. "Situated Cognition and the Culture of Learning." *Educational Researcher,* 1989, *18* (1), 32–42.

Center for Self-Sufficiency. *Homeless Families in Milwaukee After Welfare Reform.* Milwaukee, Wisc.: Center for Self-Sufficiency, 1999.

Cobb, P., and Bowers, J. "Cognitive and Situated Learning Perspectives in Theory and Practice." *Educational Researcher,* 1999, *28* (2), 4–15.

Cohen, E., and others. *Literacy and Welfare Reform: Are We Making the Connection?* National Center on Adult Literacy Technical Report no. TR94–16. Philadelphia: University of Pennsylvania, 1995. (ED 378 366)

Dirkx, J., and Prenger, S. "A Living Amoeba or a Textbook Topic? Conceptions of Integrated, Theme-Based Instruction in Adult Education." In L. Martin (ed.), *Proceedings of the Thirteenth Annual Midwest Research-to-Practice Conference in Adult, Continuing and Community Education,* Oct. 13–15. Milwaukee: University of Wisconsin-Milwaukee, 1994.

Friedlander, D., and Martinson, K. "Effects of Mandatory Basic Education for Adult AFDC Recipients." *Educational Evaluation and Policy Analysis,* 1996, *18* (4), 327–337.

Holcomb, P., Pavetti, L., Ratcliffe, C., and Reidinger, S. *Building an Employment-Focused Welfare System: Work First and Other Work-Oriented Strategies in Five States.* Washington, D.C.: U.S. Department of Health and Human Services, 1998 [http://www.urban.org/welfare/workfirs.htm].

Keeley, M. "Developing Literacy for Workers." Paper presented at the American Vocational Association Convention, Los Angeles, 1991. (ED 341 809)

Mezirow, J. "Toward a Learning Theory of Adult Literacy." *Adult Basic Education,* 1996, *6* (3), 115–126.

Murphy, G., and Johnson, A. *What Works: Integrating Basic Skills Training into Welfare-to-Work.* Washington, D.C.: National Institute for Literacy, 1998 [http://www.nifl.gov/whatworks.htm].

Palincsar, A. L. "Less-Chartered Waters." *Educational Researcher,* 1989, *18* (4), 5–7.

Resnick, L. B. "Learning In School and Out." *Educational Researcher,* 1987, *16* (9), 13–20.

Stein, S. G. *Equipped for the Future: A Reform Agenda for Adult Literacy and Lifelong Learning.* Washington, D.C.: National Institute for Literacy, 1997.

Wisconsin Works Education and Training Committee. *Building a Workforce for the Future: The Role of Education and Training in Wisconsin Works (W–2).* Madison, Wisc.: Department of Workforce Development, 1998 [http://www.Dwd.state.wi.us/desw2/Govw2etc.htm].

LARRY G. MARTIN is associate professor of adult and continuing education and department chair at the University of Wisconsin-Milwaukee.

*This chapter presents the situational-context model for
the development and delivery of adult literacy programs
within the context of the workplace.*

5

The Brave New World of Workforce Education

Eunice N. Askov, Edward E. Gordon

Welfare reform legislation, major demographic shifts in the labor market, and the continual expansion of the U.S. economy have led to major changes in American business, which has seen unemployment rates fall in many regions to twenty-five–year lows. Global competition and rapidly advancing technology have also contributed to the constant state of change. Business now desperately needs new practical strategies to fill a skills gap that is far broader than was first realized.

The skilled people most businesses now seek are the so-called knowledge workers who staff high-performance workplaces run by advanced technologies and team management. These workers need reading, writing, and math skills; computer skills, including knowledge of different software; problem-solving skills; the ability to participate in meetings; report-writing skills; the ability to read blueprints; and other skills and knowledge. These are the competencies that quality assurance programs and other performance monitors in business regard as minimal for most service or production jobs. Thus the question that confronts adult basic educators in the era of welfare reform is this: "How do we train current and former welfare recipients to find and keep jobs that meet the educational requirements of a twenty-first century business?"

Part of the answer can be found in a study by Heinrich (1996) at the University of Chicago. Heinrich examined a successful job training program for the residents of Ford Heights, Chicago's most depressed suburban community. She found that there were five major factors that contributed to people's losing their new jobs: limited work histories or no prior job experience, poor technical skills, child-care problems, a view of work as an unknown or threatening experience, and few role models to teach the behavior patterns necessary to succeed in jobs.

To overcome these problems, welfare-to-work programs need to take a holistic service approach that sequentially or concurrently provides for all necessary employment, training, and support services. The intent of this holistic service approach is to emphasize longer-term education, intensive personal coaching, and job-specific, customized training that promotes long-term job retention. Many of these useful ideas are suggested in Knell's *Learn to Earn* report (1998). Other useful and recent reports provide profiles of successful basic skills programs that are working with welfare-to-work clients (Murphy and Johnson, 1998) and suggestions for how community-level adult basic education providers can fit into the workforce development system (Jurmo, 1998).

The main objective of the coaching activity is to help each job trainee identify and work through any problems he or she may encounter during the training period. This means frequent contacts and a very hands-on approach, with coaches making phone calls or house calls after hours to ensure trainees are attending class or fulfilling job responsibilities.

Trainees may also need assistance through role playing and mock interviews, vocabulary development, guidance on hygiene and personal presentation, motivational sessions, and help with developing a resume. Additional support services might even include provision of meals, uniforms, shoes, equipment, books, child care, point-to-point transportation, medical care, and even crisis services and family counseling.

However, all these educational and support services will be of little use unless they are built around one major foundation: concurrent, effective, on-the-job training. With unemployment at low levels, business needs to use these strategies in turning to the large pool of long-term unemployed workers, to shape them into the productive knowledge workers of tomorrow. (See Gordon [1997], Gordon, Morgan, and Ponticell [1994], and Gordon, Ponticell, and Morgan [1991] for further discussions of these issues.)

Case Study

The Chicagoland Chamber of Commerce (CCC), a nonprofit economic enhancement organization, partnered with one of the authors of this chapter to provide a workforce education, welfare-to-work training program. The CCC trains groups of workers and companies through its on-the-job-training programs funded by the Job Training Partnership Act (JTPA). With the Marriott organization, we trained workers in CCC's Future Tech program for basic reading and math skills needed in the hotel chain's housekeeping positions. Another group of maids was enrolled in an English as a second language (ESL) program.

As a first step the CCC provided small-class instruction on workplace culture and appropriate behavior on the job. Once an employee began working, he or she participated in small-group tutorial classes on site twice each week for ten weeks. A specific learning curriculum that was both diagnostic and developmental was used by the instructors to individualize the tutoring. This approach emphasized a coaching or mentoring relationship with the trainee that reinforced consistent attendance in class and on the job as well as the long-term positive consequences of "learning to earn."

One of the results of the training was that their city's daily newspaper became "user-friendly" to the students. During the tutoring classes, they read help wanted ads, learning about their job requirements and specifically about hotel positions that would become available to them as they acquired more knowledge and problem-solving skills. CCC placed them at hotels that provided good, upward career ladders. However, without this workforce education program, they would not have known about higher-level jobs or how to get them.

The basic skill trainer characterized some of the training work with the following comments: "They [the students] talked about recipes and reinforcing measuring skills. The use of the newspaper to increase knowledge of current events and job responsibilities helped reinforce good basic living [and] job skills. General information of all sorts that is sometimes taken for granted by many of us was eagerly learned by these adults. Sometimes thought of as trivial information, this was found to be beneficial to these adults. They had never been exposed to or taught such knowledge."

The fact that their employer offered training that improved their quality of life had a major motivational impact on these employees. Too often, companies view unemployed individuals as high-risk candidates for employment. There are few business education programs that help anchor these adults in the foundations of effective daily functioning in a modern urban society. We believe that welfare-to-work education programs have considerable potential for teaching such lifestyle and work "anchors" and thereby building a more stable, dedicated national workforce.

The ESL students had very different experiences. Their literacy ability in their native language approached, at best, the third-grade level. Their language training focused on housekeeping vocabulary and vocabulary commonly used with hotel guests. The ESL trainer typified their work with these comments: "The ESL training provided them with a good inner feeling that each of them is capable of learning! They were surprised with their own learning ability and realized that with more exposure and practice, they could each begin to speak English. . . . This exposure to the English language, and to a learning environment, gave them an incentive to learn to communicate better."

The CCC has learned through these experiences that training must be scheduled at least partially during working hours. Students had been volunteering to attend training for an hour at the end of the workday. Many ended up with poor class attendance, which reduced individual skill gains. Also, the company learned to designate a permanent training classroom, so everyone would know where to report and acclimate to the setting. It is not recommended that the training space be moved around to whatever space is available each day.

The CCC and the participating hotels recognized the value of one-to-one tutoring or small-group instruction. They offered a prescriptive learning method that tailored the program content to each individual student's abilities. Even though these tutorial classes required a greater investment than traditional classroom instruction would have, the learning outcomes were far better, with the corollary of increased personal performance, enhanced employee motivation, and increased organizational productivity. Given these positive results, we believe this type of workforce education program can produce greater long-term employment for current and former welfare recipients than can traditional approaches to adult education. Adult educators are proving that they have a role to play in training current and former welfare recipients for the workplace. In turn, contractual work with business and industry is becoming an important source of revenue for adult educators, especially in the new arena of welfare-to-work programs. Educators are realizing that they can no longer teach basic skills in isolation—they must also ensure the transfer of those basic skills to the workplace.

Situated Learning

The concept of situated learning (Shor, 1987) has great relevance to adult literacy programs delivered in the workplace. Since instruction in this model is designed to meet learners' needs, interests, and concerns, learning is meaningful and relevant. Although the common context could be family concerns or some other issue, in the workplace it makes sense to use the context of the job as the common knowledge and experience base for the literacy program. Sticht (1987) has referred to this instructional strategy as the "functional context" approach to instruction, in which work-related basic skills are first determined and then taught using job materials, reinforcing not only work-related basic skills but also job knowledge. More recently, Sticht (1998) pointed out that the U.S. military has used this strategy since World War II. Troops in job-related skills programs feel they are getting *job* training rather than remedial or basic skills training. These troops exhibited four to five times the amount of skill improvement as did other personnel enrolled in generic skills training for the same amount of time.

Situated learning, in which instruction is contextual, based on real-world knowledge and experiences, encourages transfer of knowledge and skills from the classroom to the job. Although Mikulecky and Lloyd (1993) did not find much transfer occurring in workplace literacy programs, Askov and Brown (1991) did document transfer in a workplace literacy program for commercial truck drivers. Gershwin (1996) also found that workplace literacy instruction explicitly tailored to a functional context led to skills transfer among learners. Taylor's comprehensive manual (1998) on learning transfer in workplace education programs in Canada describes strategies and provides case studies of transfer of learning.

Preparing for Instruction. The first step in designing instruction for workforce education is to determine the goals for the program of the major stakeholders, including management, unions, workers, trainers, and human resource personnel. If a program for training welfare recipients is located in a company, program stakeholders must agree up front on the nature of the program, the target participants, what assessments will be used, how issues of confidentiality will be addressed, what resources will be available, what constraints will be faced, and the roles of each stakeholder group. Even if the program is offered at an adult education center, potential employers and unions should be involved to ensure that the program is responsive to local needs.

Frequent meetings of representatives of the stakeholder groups must be scheduled to make adjustments in the program as it is being developed so that it will meet the needs and expectations of each group. Jurmo (1991) appropriately cautions that stakeholders need to understand that basic skills programs may call for lengthy involvement—that there is no "quick fix."

The second step is to determine the jobs that will be the target of the workplace literacy program. It may be that hourly positions within certain departments will be the initial focus, especially if these positions are held by workers with low skills, or the program may be opened up to the entire plant. The next step is to determine the essential tasks of those jobs. Usually the workers themselves are the best source for determining which tasks occur often as part of the job and involve the application of literacy skills. Supervisors and trainers also can identify the essential job tasks within a department.

The functional context approach to instruction usually begins with this type of task analysis as the means of developing the curriculum for workplace literacy. The adult educator, with the cooperation of management and labor partners, studies the major tasks of the targeted jobs to determine the essential basic skills required for them, observing and interviewing experienced workers, interviewing supervisors and trainers, and collecting all written materials and information on the targeted jobs, including job descriptions, job training materials, manuals and procedures, and print and computer materials (including schematics, routing sheets, directions, and signs) used on the job. Those job-related basic skills and work materials then become the basis for the curriculum to be delivered at the workplace.

Some problems exist with this approach if instruction is focused only on specific jobs. Usually many jobs, rather than a few, are targeted within an industry. These jobs may be very different in terms of the specific basic skills required, even though they may all be under the same roof. Classes are usually scheduled, especially in manufacturing industries, so that only a few workers from each job area will miss work at one time. The instructor is thus faced with a class of workers who not only have very different jobs but also different basic skills needs and abilities within the same industry. The resources are usually not present for developing individualized curricula for the various jobs within the industry.

A solution may be to offer customized basic skills instruction that is work related and focused on the needs and materials of the workplace but not linked precisely to specific jobs. Since workplace literacy programs are often developed because jobs are changing, teaching only the basic skills associated with a specific job may not be as useful as thought initially. It makes more sense to offer more general work-related basic skills instruction that includes the workers in the decision-making process.

The workers themselves are often aware of what they need; their input can be gathered through an anonymous needs assessment conducted by the union or worker advisory group. The purpose is to determine the commonalties in the types of written and oral communication and problem-solving skills that are required for the targeted jobs. Trainers and supervisors can help add specificity to the nature of the needs of the future workplace.

In addition, the adult educator can look for general workplace literacy skills identified as necessary by the task analyses; these should be developed using work-related materials. (See Askov [1996] for suggested skills and skill standards for workplace literacy programs.) Some literacy skills that are frequently required in the workplace are

- The ability to understand technical vocabulary, including abbreviations, used in a particular industry, not only on the job but also as part of training materials, signs, bulletin boards, and employee handbooks.
- The ability to read schematic graphs, charts, tables, diagrams, blueprints, and maps used in the industry.
- The ability to follow directions or procedures, including procedural guidelines, checklists, routing sheets, and print and computer directions.
- The ability to grasp both main ideas and details, especially in training materials; usually materials used directly on the job do not require this skill, but workers are expected to have mastered the content before doing their jobs.
- Problem-solving and critical-thinking skills: the ability to identify problems and fix them quickly, or at least know whom to notify in case of a problem.
- Interpersonal and communication skills: the ability to discuss a problem with other team members (who may be from diverse cultural groups and language backgrounds) and report action taken, sometimes orally and sometimes in writing.
- Math skills, from simple measuring to complex operations needed for statistical process control.

Designing Instruction.   After identifying essential basic skills and collecting work materials, the next step is to customize as much of the instruction as possible. A variety of approaches can be used to customize instruction, including computer-assisted instruction, learner-provided and learner-generated materials, and cooperative learning exercises.

Some inexpensive software programs can be easily customized to include the technical vocabulary of a specific workplace. Some other software programs offer mini-authoring systems. The instructor can insert practice reading materials and create practice exercises from materials used on the job, in training, or in the employee handbook. These programs give immediate instruction and reinforcement in the vocabulary needed on the job, using reading materials from the workplace. (See Askov and Clark [1991] for a list of software programs and publishers. A more complete discussion of technology in adult literacy programs, including workplace literacy, may be found in Askov and Bixler [1998].)

Another solution to designing instruction for a group of workers with different jobs within the same industry is to ask the workers to bring materials from their jobs. These materials can be used as the basis for instruction, especially in designing instruction in understanding schematics, following directions, and reading for the main ideas and details.

Learner-generated materials can also be used in designing customized basic skills instruction. For example, workers can write their own job descriptions; they can also analyze the tasks related to their own jobs. This process encourages workers to analyze their strengths and weaknesses in job-related basic skills; it also encourages metacognitive (learning how to learn) abilities, helping workers to think about their own learning and skill development.

Learners can also use e-mail to communicate with others in workplace literacy programs and write about their jobs and workplaces. They can "surf the Net" to learn about issues and concerns related to employment in their business or industry as well as other work-related topics. Although this may not be a direct instructional activity, it can provide valuable practice in using newly learned language skills.

Team building is crucial in the modern industrial plant as well as in other occupations such as food and health services. Instructors can use interpersonal and communication skills needed on the job as the basis for group discussion, instruction, and practice. Cooperative learning strategies (with the instructor or experienced peer leader as facilitator) and role playing to solve work-related problems can develop higher-order and communication skills. This type of activity can form the basis of the curriculum and also focus on real problems in the workplace.

Assessment and Evaluation. Assessment and evaluation must also be planned to reflect the goals of the workplace literacy program (Askov, 1993). It is inappropriate to use general adult basic education tests to assess workers and evaluate the impact of a workplace literacy program if a customized curriculum has been developed. (See Van Horn, Carman, Askov, and Jenkins [1997] and Askov, Van Horn, and Carman [1997] for a discussion of issues surrounding assessment.) Curriculum-based assessments or criterion-referenced tests customized to the curriculum measure acquisition of skills taught using work-related materials, more accurately assess strengths and weaknesses of workers than standardized tests, and provide evidence of the impact of the program. These assessments should be designed with input from workers, trainers, and supervisors, as part of the instructional process.

Evaluation should be considered ongoing, with all stakeholders having the opportunity to suggest indicators of success. Evaluation should help shape the development of the curriculum to make it appropriate and responsive to the needs of all involved. Program expectations should be realistic; for example, a workplace literacy program is more likely to affect performance on customized assessments of basic skills than to increase productivity, quality, and safety, although the latter indicators may be important to management and may, in fact, be positively altered over time. These indicators are indirect, however, and do not directly reflect the outcomes of a workplace literacy program. (See Askov, Hoops, and Alamprese [1997] for further discussion of issues surrounding program evaluation.)

A Final Note

The workplace provides an almost ideal setting for adult learning—if all the stakeholders approach the program in good faith (McCain and Pantazis, 1997). Workers bring existing knowledge and skills to the learning situation. New workers moving off welfare can apply skills learned in their job training programs to their jobs. The integration of work-related materials and instruction in basic skills builds on workers' background of experience and knowledge while improving their abilities to use communication and computational skills more effectively in the workplace. Since such instruction is immediately applicable to learners' jobs, it can be easily transferred to the workplace, benefiting both employer and worker. Workers' needs will be further met by an ongoing program with multiple opportunities for training and education. A forward-looking curriculum that is customized to the workplace but focuses on the needs of the future rather than solely on the present will help the current workforce grow and develop. This type of program will ultimately accomplish industry's goal of creating a more productive workplace and workforce.

References

Askov, E. N. "Approaches to Assessment in Workplace Literacy Programs: Meeting the Needs of All the Clients." *Journal of Reading*, 1993, 36 (7), 550–554.

Askov, E. N. *Framework for Developing Skill Standards for Workplace Literacy*. Washington, D.C.: National Institute for Literacy, 1996.

Askov, E. N., and Bixler, B. "Transforming Adult Literacy Instruction Through Computer-Assisted Instruction." In D. Reinking, M. C. McKenna, L. D. Labbo, and R. D. Kieffer (eds.), *Literacy and Technology for the 21st Century*. Hillsdale, N.J.: Erlbaum, 1998.

Askov, E. N., and Brown, E. J. "Workplace Literacy Instruction and Evaluation: R.O.A.D. to Success." In B. L. Hayes and K. Camperell (eds.), *Yearbook of the American Reading Forum.* Vol. XI: *Literacy: International, National, State, and Local.* Logan, Utah: American Reading Forum, 1991.

Askov, E. N., and Clark, C. J. "Using Computers in Adult Literacy Instruction." *Journal of Reading,* 1991, *34* (6), 434–448.

Askov, E. N., Hoops, J., and Alamprese, J. *Assessing the Value of Workforce Training.* Washington, D.C.: National Alliance of Business, 1997.

Askov, E. N., Van Horn, B. L., and Carman, P. S. "Assessment in Adult Basic Education Programs." In M. A. Leahy and A. D. Rose (eds.), *Assessing Adult Learning in Diverse Settings: Current Issues and Approaches.* New Directions for Adult and Continuing Education, no. 75. San Francisco: Jossey-Bass, 1997.

Gershwin, M. "Workplace Learning: Reports of Change from Supervisors and Learners." *Workforce Skills; Newsletter of Educational Partnerships in Colorado.* Denver, Colo.: Community College and Occupational Education System, Fall 1996.

Gordon, E. E. "The New Knowledge Worker." *Adult Learning,* 1997, *8* (4), 14–17.

Gordon, E. E., Morgan, R. R., and Ponticell, J. A. *FutureWork, the Revolution Reshaping American Business.* New York: Praeger, 1994.

Gordon, E. E., Ponticell, J. A., and Morgan, R. R. *Closing the Literacy Gap in American Business.* Westport, Conn.: Quorum/Greenwood, 1991.

Heinrich, C. J. "The 'True Grit' Demonstration Program Evaluation Findings: One-Year Follow-up Report." Paper presented to the Cook County President's Office of Employment Training, the Private Industry Council of Suburban Cook County, and the John D. and Catherine T. MacArthur Foundation, January 1996.

Jurmo, P. "Understanding Lessons Learned in Employee Basic Skills Efforts in the U.S.: No Quick Fix." In M. C. Taylor, G. R. Lewe, and J. A. Draper (eds.), *Basic Skills for the Workplace.* Toronto: Culture Concepts, 1991.

Jurmo, P. *Integrating Adult Basic Education with Workforce Development and Workplace Change: How National-Level Policy Makers Can Help.* Monograph prepared for the U.S. Department of Education. East Brunswick, N.J.: Learning Partnerships, 1998.

Knell, S. *Learn to Earn: Issues Raised by Welfare Reform for Adult Education, Training and Work.* Literacy Leader Fellowship Program Reports. Washington, D.C.: National Institute for Literacy, 1998.

McCain, M. L., and Pantazis, C. *Responding to Workplace Change: A National Vision for a System for Continuous Learning.* Alexandria, Va.: American Society for Training and Development, 1997.

Mikulecky, L., and Lloyd, P. *The Impact of Workplace Literacy Programs: A New Model for Evaluating the Impact of Workplace Literacy Programs.* Technical Report TR93–2. Philadelphia: National Center on Adult Literacy, University of Pennsylvania, 1993.

Murphy, G., and Johnson, A. *What Works: Integrating Basic Skills Training into Welfare-to-Work.* Washington, D.C.: National Institute for Literacy, 1998 [http://www.nifl.gov/whatworks.htm].

Shor, I. *Critical Teaching and Everyday Life.* Chicago: University of Chicago Press, 1987.

Sticht, T. G. *Functional Context Education: Workshop Resource Notebook.* University Park: Institute for the Study of Adult Literacy, The Pennsylvania State University, 1987.

Sticht, T. G. "The Functional Context Approach to Adult Literacy Development." *Youth Policy,* 1998, *16* (5), 23.

Taylor, M. *Partners in the Transfer of Learning: A Resource Manual for Workplace Instructors.* Ottawa, Ontario: University of Ottawa, 1998.

Van Horn, B. L., Carman, P. S., Askov, E. N., and Jenkins, P. S. *Assessment and Adult Learners: Getting the Most from Standardized and Informal Assessment Instruments.* Final report to the Pennsylvania Department of Education (Project Number: 98–6006). University Park: Institute for the Study of Adult Literacy, The Pennsylvania State University, 1997.

EUNICE N. ASKOV is professor of education, professor in charge of adult education, and department head at The Pennsylvania State University.

EDWARD E. GORDON is president of Imperial Training Corporation and adjunct professor of business at Northwestern University.

This chapter provides a descriptive profile of several community-based programs that have responded to changes in their practice environment brought on by welfare reform and demands for workforce development.

The New Role of Community-Based Agencies

Daniel V. Folkman, Kalyani Rai

The purpose of this chapter is to describe how community-based literacy programs are responding to changes in their environment caused, in part, by recent welfare reform legislation. This inquiry represents a significant step in understanding the impact of welfare reform initiatives on community-based literacy programs. Although there is a large and growing body of literature on welfare reform in this country, there is little on the impact these reforms are having on the community-based agencies that deliver adult literacy education. The specific question addressed here is, "In what ways, if any, have the roles and functions of community-based agencies changed in the delivery of literacy programs as a result of recent changes in welfare reform legislation?"

We begin our chapter with a brief background of the welfare-to-work movement in Wisconsin, followed by a summary of the experiences of four community-based adult literacy program in Milwaukee. We then discuss how the staff at these agencies are engaged in a reassessment of their role and mission as providers of literacy education. We conclude the chapter with a framework that describes the challenges and tensions community-based agencies are negotiating in this critical reassessment period.

Background

Advocates for welfare-to-work reform assume that employment is better than relief and that getting a job takes precedence over obtaining education and training. This stands in contrast to the assumptions that drove earlier welfare policies. For example, the Family Support Act (FSA) of 1988 considered education a prerequisite to finding a good-paying job. The FSA emphasized education for welfare recipients by providing programs and services to help them graduate from high school, earn their general equivalency diploma, and enter postsecondary education or job training programs. In contrast, the Personal Responsibility and Work Opportunity Reconciliation Act (PRWORA) of 1996 shifted the emphasis of federal welfare policy toward a "Work First" approach. It mandates quick job placement and is aimed at moving recipients off the welfare caseload as quickly as possible. The policy requires that welfare recipients find a job, limits the length of time they qualify for public support, and provides for little or no support beyond job readiness training.

The state of Wisconsin has become a national leader in the welfare reform movement through its Wisconsin Works (W–2) program, which replaced Aid to Families with Dependent Children (AFDC) in the fall of 1997. The goal of W–2 is to move clients off welfare and into jobs as quickly as possible by placing them into one of four categories of jobs:

1. *Unsubsidized employment,* which includes self-employment and entrepreneurship
2. *Trial jobs,* which are subsidized by the program, with payments sent directly to employers
3. *Community service jobs,* which are designed to improve the employability of W–2 participants and may include up to ten hours of training a week aimed at getting a job
4. *W–2 transition placements,* which may include up to twelve hours of training a week aimed at eventual unsubsidized employment

Responsibility for implementing the W–2 program lies with local private or nonprofit agencies, whose staffs provide financial and employment planning and determine eligibility for support services such as day care, food stamps, medical care, job access loans, and emergency assistance.

The W–2 program's first year produced a 42 percent reduction in Wisconsin's welfare caseload. In September 1997 Wisconsin had 31,300 AFDC recipients, by December 1998 the total number of W–2 participants in all job categories was 13,093 (Institute for Wisconsin's Future, 1998a).

According to a survey report prepared in July 1998 by the Institute for Wisconsin's Future (1998b), only 53 percent of those on AFDC in September 1997 entered the W–2 program. Of those transferred to the W–2 program, about 30 percent found unsubsidized employment, 60 percent became eligible for job readiness training, and 10 percent were referred to transitional W–2 programs designed for people with severe impediments to employment. The survey results indicated that the majority of unsubsidized workers (55.2 percent) were employed in low-skill jobs with wages at or below the poverty level. Sixty-five percent of those who were assigned to community service jobs did not receive any of the training identified in the

Wisconsin Works Manual as leading to gainful employment. Of the current W–2 participants, only 17 percent have earned a high school diploma or its equivalent, and even those with a high school diploma don't have the math and reading competencies expected of a high school graduate (Governor's Wisconsin Works Education and Training Committee, 1998).

Given this highly publicized and controversial performance of W–2, what is the impact on community-based agencies that provide literacy education to adult learners? The following section describes experiences and challenges of four community-based agencies in Milwaukee.

Four Milwaukee Agencies

In developing these profiles, informal discussions were held with the directors of four community-based adult literacy programs. In each case we asked them to describe their program, the student population they serve, and the challenges they face as educators and agency administrators. We wanted to hear their story about providing literacy education in today's environment and how welfare reform is affecting their programs. All four directors were relaxed and talked candidly about their agency, its programs and strategic mission, and the challenges they face in terms of reaching and retaining students, recruiting volunteer tutors, and securing resources. Three interviews were completed, each approximately an hour and a half long. A profile of each agency was drafted and sent to the director as a check on accuracy and to elicit additional comments and clarifications and their approval for publication. The interview process for one agency consisted of three separate meetings with the director and her staff. Our interview session was part of their staff meetings. They used our questions to frame a reflective dialogue about their program and the future direction of their agency.

The approach of combining unstructured interviews, informal discussions, and feedback sessions represents our effort to describe the context within which these agencies are operating and to validate our interpretation of their response to the challenges they face. Our intent in writing these profiles is to reveal a set of themes that describe how community-based agencies are responding to their changing world, including W–2 reforms.

Journey House. This is a neighborhood-based multiservice agency located in a culturally mixed neighborhood on Milwaukee's south side. Established in 1969, Journey House provides a range of adult education programs, including adult basic education (ABE), GED programs, and English as a second language (ESL) programs. The agency also provides parenting classes, hands-on computer literacy education, job training, and placement services. On-site child care and transportation services for participants are also provided. These services continue to be available to participants who have been placed in jobs and who need day care and transportation during their first weeks of employment. Journey House currently serves 539 adult learners: 58 percent Hispanic, 16 percent African American, 2 percent

Native American, and 24 percent white. Out of this total, 114, or 21 percent, are part of the W–2 program, and all but two are female single parents.

What has been the impact of welfare reform on Journey House and its adult education programs? This question was asked of Michelle Bria, the executive director. The challenge, she responded, is to find a reasonable balance between meeting the basic academic needs of adult learners while at the same time helping them find and keep a decent-paying job. To accomplish this end, Journey House continues to provide its core academic programs in ABE, GED, and ESL. The curriculum in these areas has not changed as a result of welfare reform.

What is new, Bria explained, is a series of programs that Journey House has developed over the past several years that focus on job readiness training, coupled with job placement and retention. Job readiness involves training in both soft and hard skills. Soft skills include preparing resumes, developing interviewing skills, time management skills, and understanding the values, norms, and expectations of the workplace. Hard-skill training entails an introduction to computer skills, along with learning popular software applications. Journey House recognizes that making the transition to work involves more than just skill training. It involves translating the workplace culture into the language of the participant. Accordingly, participants tour their future worksites and talk to the employer and other workers to see first-hand what is involved in going to work. Journey House staff remain involved with the participants during the first days, weeks, and months of their employment to provide support and resolve difficulties that arise during the transition period. Journey House also provides a job placement service for the adult learners in its programs. As a result, 102 adult learners have been placed in jobs over the past twelve months.

Job placement is only part of the agency's goal, Bria explained. Job retention is equally important. Toward this end Journey House has developed programs that address two major barriers to successful employment: child care and transportation. Accordingly, day care is available to parents attending adult education programs and continues to be available to participants who have found recent employment. Also, Journey House maintains a sixteen-passenger van that provides transportation services. The van picks up the family in the morning, drops the children at day care, takes the mother to work, and picks everyone up at the end of the day. This service is guaranteed for three weeks after being placed in a job. This allows sufficient time for the first paycheck to arrive so that a bus pass can be purchased, a car pool arranged, or other transportation found. Journey House maintains a mobility management counselor who works with the newly hired participant to develop a personal transportation plan to ensure that transportation problems are not a reason for missing work.

The mission of Journey House is to meet the basic adult education needs of neighborhood residents. This focus is the foundation for the agency's collaborative relationship with United Migrant Opportunity Services (UMOS), an agency responsible for moving W–2 clients from welfare to work. The financial employment planner (FEP) refers W–2 clients to Journey House for placement in community service jobs, enrollment in its eight-week job readiness training program and related services, or both. The two agencies work together to ensure that work assignments and class schedules are coordinated. From the beginning, Journey House staff remain focused on the educational needs of the W–2 clients. In fact, the job readiness training and associated services just described are seen as strategies to keep the learner engaged in education after employment has been secured. The idea is to help the learner find a job first, and then figure out what it takes to keep him or her in school. To a great extent, job retention and promotion result from continuous learning and self-development.

Journey House enjoys a good collaborative relationship with UMOS, which is one of Milwaukee's five W–2 agencies. The two agencies are working together in designing new programs and seeking joint funding, including surplus W–2 funds. An example is a newly created program aimed at reaching noncustodial parents (usually fathers). The goal is to keep the father continuously employed for one year and to do whatever it takes to work with him to accomplish this end. The program combines mentoring with a case management approach to ensure that each individual will have someone supporting him throughout the year. A coach is assigned to fifteen fathers and is available on-call to work with them to address work-related issues and general life problems. For example, coaches arrange family counseling, advise clients on child custody issues, help with legal interventions, and generally help smooth out problems that contribute to stress and job loss. Funding has been secured for a two-year pilot program that will include not only Journey House and UMOS but also three other community-based organizations. The design of this project, coupled with the commitment of Journey House and the three other organizations, has encouraged UMOS to invest a substantial part of its $1 million surplus in its implementation.

Literacy Services of Wisconsin (LSW). This is a privately funded organization located near downtown Milwaukee. Established in 1965, the agency began as a church-based program with the mission of providing free literacy education to all comers. Today the religious affiliation is gone, but the mission remains the same. More than seven hundred adult students enroll annually in LSW's programs. The only cost to the students is approximately $22, which covers the price of books and materials. Seventy percent of the students are enrolled in basic adult education, 20 percent in GED instruction, and 10 percent in ESL instruction. Instruction in LSW consists mostly of one-on-one tutoring, which is supported by a network of more than four hundred volunteers drawn from the greater Milwaukee area. Students commit to three hours of instruction per week. The student population is evenly divided between women and men. The majority of students are African American, followed by Hispanic, Asian, and white. LSW is part of a network of twenty-six satellite centers, which it supports through tutor training and recruitment. These network centers are located in Milwaukee and surrounding counties. More than six hundred students have received instruction at these centers, from 350 volunteer tutors. The organization does not receive government or United Way funding. Rather, financial support is secured through a mix of personal donations, private foundation grants, and corporate gifts.

What has been the impact of W–2 reform on LSW? This question was asked of Jeff Martinka, LSW's executive director. He responded that there has been little, if any, direct impact on the agency and its programs that can be directly attributed to W–2. He added, however, that gauging this impact is difficult, because students are not asked if they are participating in W–2. The assumption is that most students are not, since LSW does not work directly with agencies that provide community service jobs. Additionally, its curriculum doesn't include job-related training as defined by W–2's policies and regulations.

Still, Martinka explained, LSW is responding to major trends in the environment, which most certainly include W–2. The most striking challenge has been a significant drop in student contact hours over the past four years. In 1995, student contact hours reached a peak at over nine hundred hours per month. In subsequent years this number dropped significantly. In 1998, student contact hours averaged approximately five hundred hours per month. Martinka sites three factors that contributed to this drop: the very low unemployment rate during this period, the limited time available to W–2 participants for education, and the fact that Milwaukee's low-income population was moving out of the central city neighborhood.

In response, LSW has increased its evening and weekend hours to better accommodate the working student. Most importantly, LSW has launched an aggressive marketing and outreach campaign that includes tracking student recruitment patterns, participation levels, and learner outcomes. Activities aimed at recruiting both students and volunteers include a series of new bookmarks and posters, radio advertising, and breakfast briefings for community and corporate sponsors. LSW is also planning to initiate its own Internet site and host an annual open house. The results are encouraging. Student contact hours increased by nearly 40 percent in the first two months in 1999, surpassing the seven hundred mark.

In addition to these marketing efforts, LSW has added a series of programs to its basic curriculum. These include group essay classes, small-group instruction in life skills, a family literacy program, and self-guided computer-based instruction in basic academic skills and keyboarding. Also, free day care services are provided for students while they study at the LSW center.

Finally, LSW is adding a job readiness program to its mix of educational services. This program will help students prepare resumes, write cover letters, and practice interpersonal skills needed for successful interviewing, getting hired, and staying employed. Martinka emphasizes that this addition to the curriculum is not related to W–2. Rather, it is something that students need generally and is intended only as a complement to the core curriculum; it does not represent a shift in focus away from basic literacy education.

In short, Martinka emphasized, LSW and its network of satellite sites is unique in serving nearly one thousand students annually and maintaining a volunteer base of more than seven hundred tutors. Funding is relatively secure. As a result, the agency remains committed to literacy education and has not broadened its services beyond its original mission. The greatest challenge facing the agency is recruiting students and volunteers. Recent marketing and outreach efforts have produced a significant increase in instructional hours, which reflect both student and volunteer time. W–2 has had little, if any, direct impact on LSW's services, and there are no plans to integrate job readiness, placement, and retention programs and related services as a result of welfare reform in Wisconsin.

Milwaukee Achiever Program (MAP). This is a not-for-profit faith-based agency created more than fifteen years ago through a collaboration of three local colleges: Alverno, Cardinal Stritch, and Mount Mary. The founding vision of these three colleges was to serve Milwaukee's economically and educationally disenfranchised population.

MAP's long-standing mission has been to provide adult learners with preparatory and developmental instruction in ABE, ESL, GED, and citizenship skills, with individualized instruction, flexible scheduling, and a sliding fee scale. Instruction is delivered through an extensive network of approximately 240 volunteers, who provide one-on-one tutoring and instruction in small-group settings. In recent years MAP has added computer literacy training to its curriculum and created the JobLink program, which provides custom-designed classes offered on-site for private companies on a contractual basis. MAP is currently serving over four hundred adult learners, with 70 percent taking ESL classes, 20 percent enrolled in BAE classes, and 10 percent working toward their GED. Programs are offered in three locations to ensure easy access by adult learners, who are nearly evenly divided between women and men. A majority of the learners are Hispanic (53 percent); the rest are African American (27 percent), white (13 percent), and Asian (8 percent). Finally, cross-cultural appreciation is an important part of MAP's mission. This is achieved through the supportive relationships created between the learners, who come from a variety of racial, ethnic, and cultural backgrounds, and the MAP volunteers, who are predominately white and middle-class and live throughout the greater Milwaukee area. The MAP archives are filled with rich and touching stories of long-term friendships and deep personal learning that has occurred between the adult students and volunteers.

What has been the impact of welfare reform on MAP? This question was asked of Sister Agnes-Marie Henkel, executive director, and her staff.

Most of the impact of welfare reform has been felt at one of the three MAP sites. This site has a predominantly African American population that was on AFDC at the time of W–2. The other two sites have mostly Hispanic, eastern European, and Asian learners who are mostly new immigrants with little or no welfare experience. In most cases they were either working or supported by an extended family and community network. Consequently, the overall impact of welfare reform on MAP has been minimal. Only a small number of learners are identified as W–2 participants. Furthermore, MAP's literacy curriculum is focused solely on academic readiness and life-long learning, not job readiness or job training. Changes in schedules to include more evening and weekend tutoring and small-group sessions are occurring at all three MAP sites. These scheduling changes have, in turn, affected the volunteer base, since many were comfortable with weekday sessions and now must accommodate evening and weekend assignments. This change has also triggered concern among some volunteers about driving into the central city after dark or on weekends. This later concern is a particular issue for one site, which is located in a light industrial area where there is little activity at night and on the weekends.

Although this change in scheduling has some volunteers concerned, Sister Henkel points out that adding evening and weekend sessions has not added significantly to the normal challenge of recruiting and retaining volunteers. Most volunteers are recruited through city and suburban congregations. Over the past several years, MAP has turned to Milwaukee area businesses as a source of volunteer help. Special partnerships are arranged with companies, through which groups of employees volunteer together, making their service a community effort.

A major challenge that is only partially related to welfare reform is the highly variable participation rates among the adult learners. All students come to the program with the goals of learning to read, write, and speak English as well as to earn their GED. Some also come with other, very specific objectives, such as learning long division, learning how to use a ruler, or learning how to read simple street signs. Once the specific goal is met, the student stops coming. Other learners start a program but drop out because of changes in their work, family, or living arrangements or for other reasons. Many of these learners return when their life situations again become more balanced.

At one point MAP thought that W–2 would be a source of student referrals, but this has not been the case. In spite of numerous attempts to establish a contract with different W–2 agencies in Milwaukee, none of these agencies have shown interest in contracting with MAP. Sister Henkel and her staff remain frustrated as a result of this situation.

Rather than seeking formal ties with a W–2 agency, MAP has embarked on an alternative strategy—to expand its existing JobLink program, which seeks job training contracts with area businesses. A recent experience illustrates both the opportunity and the challenges that lie along this path. Early discussion with one local midsized firm had shown promise. The company had an impressive employee training program. Although this training program was envisioned as being for all employees, it was used mostly by middle and upper management, with little or no support for entry-level workers, especially those needing basic skills training or ESL instruction. The company organized its own literacy and ESL program and expected employees to attend after working hours or on their days off, without compensation. MAP discussed the disparity and shortsighted nature of the company's training policy with management and convinced them that not only should all workers be given an opportunity to participate in ABE programs, but the company should also pay them wages during training. Further, it was proposed that supervisors participate in the training program, since they are responsible for continuing the learning process once students return to the shop floor. How can supervisors perform this function, MAP representatives asked, if they don't understand or appreciate what is going on in the learning sessions? The result was a new contract with this company. The training program started in February 1999, with employees paid for their learning time and supervisors part of the planning process.

College in the Community is another innovation in which both MAP and Journey House are participating. Mount Mary is a small Catholic liberal arts college and one of MAP's founding institutions. The college and MAP are offering a series of classes in business English, computer keyboarding, and software applications. These classes are designed for both MAP students and residents in the surrounding neighborhoods. Students who complete this instruction earn credits that can be used toward a degree from Mount Mary if they are later accepted through the school's normal application process. Child care is provided through a certified provider. (This provider, incidentally, is enrolled in the MAP GED program, and she currently owns and operates two child-care centers.)

YWCA Vel Phillips Adult Learning Center. The YWCA Education and Employment Enrichment Program is operated through the Vel Phillips Adult Learning Center. It is located in the central city of Milwaukee and serves a primarily African American population. As one of the five W–2 agencies in Milwaukee, the YWCA operates in partnership with Kaiser Group, Inc., and Clinical Network Resource (CNR) Health, Inc., as a W–2 program provider for Region 1, which is located in the central part of Milwaukee. The Vel Phillips Adult Learning Center works in close coordination with the YWCA to ensure that education, employment, and other support services are provided to W–2 participants.

The center serves a total of 471 adult learners annually, and 85 percent of the total are W–2 participants. The student enrollment has increased by 150 percent since the beginning of W–2. Nearly all learners are women between the age of twenty-two and thirty. The program offers ABE and GED instruction, job readiness training, and brush-up instruction in math, computer science, and reading. The program staff develops a personal education plan with each student, based on his or her skill level.

What has been the impact of W–2 reform on the YWCA Vel Phillips Adult Learning Center Program? This question was asked of Grace Bottoni, the program director. One major change brought about by W–2 has been a reordering of the program's priorities. For example, the core instructional time for basic skills has been reduced from four hours to two hours per week, whereas sessions devoted to job training and brush-up instruction have increased from twice to four times a month. The regular four-hour basic skill program has been squeezed into a two-hour session to make time for job readiness training. After one year, the program boasted the following successes: a majority of the W–2 participants in the program were reading at a fourth- to sixth-grade level, 118 had increased their reading level, 54 had found jobs or improved their job status, and 14 had received their GED.

In response to the need for more accountability under W–2, the agency has developed a new data tracking system. A computerized time card now tracks W–2 participants throughout the YWCA's W–2 programs. This system has increased the efficiency of the Vel Phillips Center's data tracking and has saved the center's staff a tremendous amount of time formerly devoted to daily data reporting.

The Vel Phillips Center coordinates its programs with other YWCA support services, including child-care services, case management, substance abuse programs, youth development programs, counseling services, and career guidance. YWCA refers W–2 participants to Vel Phillips for placement in community service jobs or enrollment in ABE, GED, and job readiness programs. The Vel Phillips and YWCA staffs work together to design education and employment training for each W–2 participant.

A major part of the YWCA's W–2 strategy has been to create its own business that will provide opportunities for W–2 participants to earn livable wages and receive on-site job training. Accordingly, a newly developed YWCA plastics reprocessing company—Generation 2 Plastics—serves as a community service job site for W–2 participants.

A major challenge for the Vel Phillips center is to find a balance between meeting the core academic needs of learners and helping them find gainful employment. Its academic curriculum is focused on ABE and GED instruction, coupled with job training that involves preparing resumes, developing job interview skills, and attending time management and motivation seminars. As the agency continues to expand its tutoring and literacy programs, it faces the need to increase its effort to recruit and train volunteers. It is also facing the need to expand its facility in the near future to accommodate the growing number of participants being referred by the YWCA. The biggest challenge facing the agency is to develop its partnerships with other agencies that have the capacity to serve adult learners with severe social and learning disabilities. As the program continues to expand, the agency also faces a challenge to secure continuous funding. The program's success has been attributed to a small group of dedicated staff who benefit from their close association with the YWCA of greater Milwaukee and its track record of service to Milwaukee's central city community.

Discussion

The case studies described in this chapter capture the tensions that exist within a community-based organization as it struggles to provide adult literacy education in today's economic, social, and political environment. The literature on welfare-to-work programs offers a prescription for success: integrate basic literacy education with job readiness, placement, and retention programs coupled with personal and family support services (Cohen, 1998). This is easier said than done. Our interviews with agency directors and staff indicate that following this advice means undergoing a critical reassessment of one's role and mission as a provider of literacy education.

The academic literature views this discussion as a philosophical discourse on the purpose of literacy education: should it fulfill a vocational, liberal, humanist, or liberatory mission (Quigley, 1997)? For the practitioner, the issue is not simply adhering to a basic philosophical principle but rather striking a balance between the multiple challenges depicted in Figure 6.1. To survive, the practitioner must negotiate tradeoffs. Being learner-focused means finding a balance between teaching for personal growth and development and training for employment. Being agency-focused means finding the necessary resources to run an organization while seeking ways to add new and different services, either within the agency itself or in collaboration with one's competitors. The objective of the collaboration is to create a micro safety net for the learner.

In effect, the nation's community-based agencies, like many of the adult learners they serve, are negotiating their own transformation in perspective. They are reassessing their basic values and assumptions about the purpose of literacy education and their long-term strategic plan as organizations. In the process, decisions are being made and risks taken. Some organizations are choosing to remain true to their historic mission, which often means remaining focused on the learner and her or his educational needs. Others are finding ways to incorporate into their mission a range of services that will transform their agency, making literacy education an integral part of a more comprehensive agenda. Either way, community-based organizations must find new and creative teaching methods, including computer-assisted instruction; market their programs, in an effort to recruit and retain both students and volunteers; and connect their literacy education to other needs, including the welfare-to-work transition, personal development, and even community empowerment (Taylor, 1991).

Figure 6.1. Challenges in Delivering Community-Based Adult Literacy Education

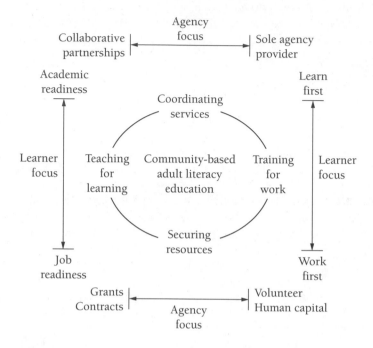

Challenges and Implications

What has been the impact of welfare-to-work reforms on community-based organizations delivering literacy education? Our discussions with agency directors and staff suggest that W–2 reforms in Milwaukee are having an indirect impact on agencies. It is difficult to gauge this impact on agencies that are not working closely with Milwaukee's W–2 agencies. Other agencies, for the most part, do not identify their learners as welfare recipients, W–2 clients, or community service workers. What these agencies are responding to are the more general pervasive trends occurring in the economy—specifically, the record low unemployment that has now persisted for a number of years. Thus many adult learners are now finding employment, which means literacy programs must adjust their curricula and schedules to accommodate a growing number of working students regardless of whether or not they are W–2 recipients. To attract and keep these students, community-based agencies are adding evening and weekend programs, providing day care, and reaching out to employers in an effort to add workplace literacy programs to their mix of educational programs and services. Add the social and political rhetoric associated with welfare reform, and you have an environment that emphasizes job training, placement, and retention over basic education. These goals are competing to become the central mission of most adult literacy programs and the locus of commitment for agency staff and volunteers. This situation describes a highly conflicted environment in which the community-based organization must operate. Accordingly, there are several major challenges facing community-based literacy programs. Figure 6.1 depicts these challenges as a set of two dichotomies that pull agencies and their staffs in different directions: the mandate to teach for learning versus the mandate to train for work, and the need to coordinate services versus the need to secure resources. The divergent points of these dichotomies are described more fully in the following paragraphs.

Teaching for Learning. How can agencies balance students' need to learn academic skills with their need for job readiness training? The answer is to embrace a more holistic curriculum that places literacy education on a continuum that includes job readiness, employment and career development, more advanced training, and higher education, coupled with personal, family, and community empowerment. From this perspective, the teaching and learning environment is no longer limited to the classroom or to one-on-one relationships with volunteer tutors but extends to include the workplace, the home, and the entire community.

Training for Work. Which comes first, education or employment? Changes in welfare reform mandate work over learning. Students who were previously on welfare must now accommodate competing work, family, and school schedules. Accordingly, many students are dropping out or delaying their education. The challenge for the community-based organization is to modify its curriculum and program schedule to accommodate the working and job-seeking student.

Coordinating Services. How can agencies develop an educational delivery system that integrates academic instruction with support services such as day care, job placement, transportation, personal and family counseling, legal aid, and others? The challenge is to reassess the role and function of the community-based literacy program. There is increasing pressure to shift from being a sole provider of educational programs to being a partner within a network of agencies that is capable of addressing the multiple and competing needs of the adult learner.

Securing Resources. What is the product, and where are the resources? Community-based organizations are under pressure not only to modify their curricula, adjust their schedules, and coordinate their educational services with other agencies but also to develop a marketing approach to program development and delivery, to ensure their own survival. The trick is to create innovative programs that deliver in terms of student academic achievement and employment while remaining focused on quality service, customer satisfaction, and just-in-time delivery. The challenge is to develop an entrepreneurial approach that will move the enterprise from a specialty shop in literacy education to a retail distributor of educational programs and support services. The challenge, in effect, is to relocate the business from classrooms in the church basement to the mall or shop floor.

Conclusions

The agency directors and staff we interviewed were concerned about maintaining their identity as education providers while balancing the dichotomies just described. Today's answer is only a temporary solution, because circumstances will surely change. One trend is clear, however: the community-based organization must learn to function within a network of stakeholders that includes not only learners, volunteers, and financial contributors but also businesses as consumers and other program providers as collaborating partners. Learning to survive and grow in this multifaceted environment is the ultimate challenge facing agency directors and staff. Although none of those we interviewed had a blueprint for success, all were confident in their ability to invent solutions as they go.

References

Cohen, M. "Education and Training Under Welfare Reform." *Welfare Information Network Issue Notes*, 1998, 2 (2), 3.

Governor's Wisconsin Works Education and Training Committee. *Recommendations and Action Plan: A Report by the Governor's Wisconsin Works (W–2) Education and Training Committee.* Madison: Governor's Wisconsin Works Education and Training Committee, 1998.

Institute for Wisconsin's Future. *Transitions to W–2: The First Six Months of Welfare Replacement.* Milwaukee: Institute for Wisconsin's Future, 1998a.

Institute for Wisconsin's Future. *The W–2 Job Path: An Assessment of the Employment Trajectory of W–2 Participants in Milwaukee.* Milwaukee: Institute for Wisconsin's Future, 1998b.

Murphy, G., and Johnson, A. *What Works: Integrating Basic Skills Training into Welfare-to-Work.* Washington, D.C.: National Institute for Literacy, 1998 [http://www.nifl.gov/whatworks.htm].

Quigley, A. *Rethinking Literacy Education: The Critical Need for Practice-Based Change.* San Francisco: Jossey-Bass, 1997.

Taylor, M. "Adult Basic Education." In A. Knox (ed.), *Handbook of Adult Education.* San Francisco: Jossey-Bass, 1991.

DANIEL V. FOLKMAN *is associate professor and chair, Center for Urban Community Development, University Outreach, University of Wisconsin-Milwaukee.*

KALYANI RAI *is assistant professor, Center for Urban Community Development, University Outreach, University of Wisconsin-Milwaukee.*

This chapter explores the implications for literacy educators of changes in curricula and program implementation stemming from welfare reform and workforce development.

New Skills for Literacy Educators

John M. Dirkx

Over the last fifteen years, the field of adult literacy and basic education has increasingly reflected a concern in the greater society over issues of work and intergenerational literacy and welfare. Yet this shift has not, for the most part, been attached to or part of a larger policy context. Discussions about adult education and training have touched on concerns about our global competitiveness; the need for a viable, efficient, educated, and well-trained workforce; and the effects on children of being raised in the suffocating throes of poverty. But in terms of policy, these discussions rarely went beyond the creation of demonstration projects, specially funded programs, and a few state initiatives. In many respects, the federal initiatives that created and sustained these programs for a time were not much more than Band-Aids placed on what many perceived to be gaping wounds in our social and economic fabric.

With the passage of the Personal Responsibility and Work Opportunity Reconciliation Act (PRWORA) in 1996 (Public Law 104–193), however, adult basic and literacy education found itself irrevocably bound up with a major social policy. This legislation was passed with the intent of making sweeping and widespread changes in the U.S. welfare system. Whether we agree with the direction in which these social reforms are taking us as a society, there is little doubt that the future practice of adult literacy education is now deeply intertwined with these new policy initiatives. And this marriage, as uncomfortable as it may be for many of us, will require substantial rethinking of our practice—its basic tenants, its philosophical perspectives, and its models of curricula and instruction.

The purpose of this chapter is to address how welfare reform is requiring adult literacy educators to reexamine the fundamental beliefs and values that guide their practice and reassess which skills are needed in their

NEW DIRECTIONS FOR ADULT AND CONTINUING EDUCATION, no. 83, Fall 1999   © Jossey-Bass Publishers profession. I will first make a case for the changing nature of curricula and programming in adult literacy and basic education, stemming from an increased emphasis on job placement and workforce development. Then I will explore the implications of these changes for the role of the literacy educator. I will suggest the need to reshape what we consider to be the practice of adult literacy education, focusing on what educators need to know, what they should be able to do, and how we will make sense of adult literacy education in this new "Work First" environment.

Linking Adult Basic and Literacy Education with Welfare Reform

The 1996 federal welfare reform act (Public Law 104–193) significantly altered the political and social context for the practice of adult literacy and basic education. At one level, this new legislation clearly emphasizes moving individuals off of public assistance and into work, and it minimizes the role of adult education and training in this process. In this so-called Work First environment, welfare recipients are required to look for and locate work *before* they pursue education and training (Knell, 1998). The wording of this act suggests certain conditions under which education and training may be permissible prior to working, such as for individuals who are determined to be not yet ready for a job. Even then, the emphasis is on short-term education and training—only what is needed for welfare recipients to engage in paid work. For the most part, welfare recipients are not encouraged to seek out long-term education and training before they find a job. Some scholars suggest that in this Work First environment, women are actually being pushed out of educational programs in favor of low-paying, subsistence jobs (Sparks, 1999).

Yet, evidence suggests that the new welfare legislation implicitly increases emphasis on literacy and basic education (Knell, 1998). The various ways in which this seeming paradox manifests itself are complex and addressed in the various chapters of this sourcebook. Low levels of educational achievement and skill are linked with low economic states and unemployment. As Martin and Fisher (1998) point out, "Welfare recipients have low educational skills; nearly half of adults on welfare do not have a high school diploma or GED. Recipients' level of educational skill is correlated with length of time on welfare . . . [and the] educational level of welfare recipients is closely linked to their income level" (p. 129). (See Chapter Three for more details on research involving low-literate welfare recipients.)

Given the overall educational achievement and literacy level of the majority of individuals receiving public assistance, adult education and training has to be viewed as a necessary and essential component of any effective and comprehensive welfare-to-work system. Adult education and training represent critical processes that will provide these individuals with a chance to become economically self-sufficient as well as to be able to fully participate politically in civil society. In their report on the relationship between literacy and dependency, Barton and Jenkins (1995) conclude that dependency on welfare can be reduced by increasing the literacy level of the general population, to reduce the risk of individuals' falling into dependency, and of those on welfare, to help them become more financially self-sufficient. Others, such as Freire (1998) and Fingeret and Drennon (1997) demonstrate how literacy practices are inextricably linked with sociocultural and political empowerment. Despite the Work First philosophy of many welfare reform initiatives, policy in many states suggests at least an implicit recognition of education and training as vital components of the long-term success of such programs.

Efforts have been made over the last five years to connect work-focused welfare reform programs with adult literacy education and training. This effort represents a trend that began in the early 1980s and, in the 1990s, has increasingly linked adult literacy education with economic and family welfare issues. In our current socioeconomic and political climate, numerous policies and programs have emerged to "reform" welfare. Adult literacy practice is viewed by many as important not only to our nation's ability to remain globally competitive but also to resolving what many feel are inherent, long-term problems with welfare programs. These evolving views of adult literacy practice are taking place within a context of rapid technological change and increasing cultural diversity within our adult population.

Thus it is clear that, in a strange and somewhat paradoxical way, the practice of adult basic and literacy education is intimately intertwined with this new Work First environment. The context for adult literacy education is undergoing rapid change, and with it are changing the knowledge and skills practitioners need to be effective. This new context will require adult educators to think about their practice in quite different ways from how they did in the past and to learn new skills that will be needed in this environment.

Implications of the Work First Environment for Adult Literacy Education

Martin and Fisher (1998) clearly point out that welfare reform initiatives sweeping the country call into question a "business as usual" approach in adult literacy education. In the Work First environment, they say, "traditional literacy programs are a low priority. Welfare recipients are directed to participate in learning programs . . . that more effectively assist them in meeting the employment requirements of local employers. Any training must be tied directly to jobs obtainable after brief preparation" (p. 128). Despite the minimizing of adult education and training within this Work First environment, a general consensus is emerging that this new policy initiative will actually increase the need and demand for adult literacy education (Murphy and Johnson, 1998). But this increased demand is predicated on a fundamental assumption: that the nature and delivery of adult literacy education programs will change dramatically.

As analyses of exemplary programs have demonstrated, adult literacy education will need to be shorter, more intensive, and more closely grounded in work and training than in the past (Murphy and Johnson, 1998). A recent study on the impact of the Work First philosophy on family literacy programs illustrates in a concrete way the nature of the changes welfare reform is bringing about in adult basic and literacy education (Alamprese and Voight, 1998). Observations from pilot projects set up in 1997 by the National Center for Family Literacy noted major changes in family literacy programs in three areas: duration of services, curricular content, and program processes. The Work First philosophy has forced these programs to shorten their curricula and focus more specifically on job readiness skills. They are also supplementing their face-to-face instruction with off-site activities aimed at preparing their learners for work. This requires adult educators to coordinate their programs and services with local employers and community agencies.

The curricula of these pilot programs are also being radically changed, with much more emphasis on work readiness and career awareness than before. Educators are facing the need to teach basic skills in the context of work and also to foster job awareness and specific workplace skills. As a result, this shift in curricular focus has brought about specific changes in the kinds of activities used in the adult education component of these programs. Among activities now being incorporated into adult basic education programs are job shadowing, mentoring, and specific work experiences.

These dramatic shifts in program curricula and pedagogical processes have challenged the educators staffing these programs to use their time with adult learners in a creative and optimal manner. Considerable tension remains between these various program elements, the goal of fostering literacy to support learners in their roles as parents and active participants in civil society, and other goals that focus more specifically on the world of work. Educators are faced with an ongoing need to hold these tensions in check and balance potentially competing program goals. These new curricular and programmatic needs require skills and knowledge that were not necessarily required of educators before the advent of the Work First environment.

The process of linking welfare reform to adult literacy reflects several characteristics critical to the work of adult educators. Although some of these characteristics may be viewed as extensions of or elaborations on what some programs have been doing for years, the changes suggested here will have sweeping implications for adult literacy education as a field of practice. Building on earlier works in this area (Cohen and others, 1995; Imel, 1995a, 1995b; Pauly, Long, and Martinson, 1992; Reder and Wikelund, 1994), I focus here on the following tasks required of literacy education planners and practitioners in today's environment:

- Designing and tailoring programs to the specific needs of clients
- Fostering strong, working collaborative relationships and partnerships with welfare and Work First agencies, community agencies, and employers
- Focusing on comprehensive outcomes for participants
- Planning and designing programs and curricula that are holistic and fully integrated with work, family, and community contexts
- Developing systems of accountability that clearly demonstrate the effects of program activities
- Providing for continuous staff development

Designing Programs to Address Participant Needs. Welfare recipients bring to adult literacy education a wide diversity and a range of prior experiences with educational agencies, employers, family contexts, and so on. These experiences shape their goals, hopes, dreams, and aspirations as well as their attitudes toward and expectations about education. The level of education, knowledge, and skills they bring to their learning varies considerably. In addition to these education-related variables, a host of other issues must be considered for individuals in welfare-to-work programs. To help themselves compete for decent jobs that pay a living wage, many participants are looking for assistance with job skills. Obtaining employment evokes, for some, concerns related to the overall well-being of their children. In addition to possible anxiety over the need to find safe and acceptable child care, some participants also may worry about finding transportation to and from their educational program, work, and child-care locations. Others face problems within their communities—such as lack of housing, troubling relationships with landlords, or lack of access to decent medical care—that require their political involvement or engagement.

Each program participant differs with respect to the degree to which these issues represent salient dimensions of his or her world. Adult literacy programs need to be cognizant of these various issues and create educational plans and designs that address them. To be effective in helping participants acquire the skills and knowledge needed to obtain decent employment, adult literacy practitioners must attend to this diverse array of needs. Many practitioners previously defined the scope of their work within the limits of the classrooms in which they taught. The Work First environment, however, calls for an expansion of this scope and a broadened understanding of what is expected and required of literacy programs and practitioners. Practitioners will need to be more proactive in trying to understand factors that contribute to absences or attrition among their students. This information should be used to address whatever program activities or structures may be contributing to low participation rates. Adult literacy programs may very well need to expand the types of services they provide. In addition to educating their students, practitioners will find themselves involved in career counseling and job-search assistance, setting up child care, and coordinating transportation.

These additional activities will require a redefinition of the practitioner's role, requiring new skills and knowledge once thought to be outside the purview of the classroom teacher. Although some of these new responsibilities will fall to administrative personnel, classroom teachers will need to develop more knowledge of and skill in additional areas, such as career preparation. Strategies and techniques commonly used to foster acquisition of basic skills will not necessarily be useful in helping students search for a job, for example. Practitioners will need to expand their role to include career or job counseling, and they will need to develop the knowledge and skills to effectively perform that service. Many practitioners will need to develop counseling strategies and skills as well. Practitioners not working within a family literacy model or framework will need to think more holistically and systemically about their students' home contexts. Although I would not necessarily advocate that all adult literacy programs become family literacy programs, this model may help more traditional programs better address their students' needs and concerns related to the well-being of their children.

Given the short-term nature of education and training in a Work First environment, it is critical that adult literacy practitioners and programs assume a broad, holistic perspective on the lives of their students and tailor their services as much as possible to address their students' needs. In itself, this goal will require practitioners to expand their roles and develop new knowledge and skills previously considered outside the scope of their work.

Those adult literacy programs that have been successful at helping welfare recipients have integrated basic skills instruction with occupational training and have tailored themselves to participants' specific needs and challenges. Adult literacy and education programs should address noneducational barriers, such as low self-esteem, unstable housing, and severe family problems, and integrate adult literacy instruction with the education of the adult learner's children (Cohen and others, 1995).

Fostering Strong, Working Collaborative Relationships and Partnerships. Work First environments, almost by definition, are reshaping the relationships adult literacy programs have with government, community, and employer groups. There is considerable pressure to revise curricula of basic skills programs to more effectively address the needs of adults to obtain and hold a job. In addition, area employers are seeking individuals with employable skills who are "workplace ready." Both the needs of the adults coming to these programs and the area agencies who represent potential employers are having a significant influence on adult literacy and basic skills curricula.

But effective curricular changes and revisions cannot be made in the absence of substantial discussion and dialogue among the various groups who have a stake in these programs' outcomes. In addition to learners, these stakeholders include education professionals, social services agencies, employment and training agencies, and employers. In the past, many programs have invited representatives from stakeholder groups to participate on advisory boards or on committees. Yet, advisory board members often felt more like recipients of information than active players in the formation of program policies and curricula. In interviews conducted as part of program evaluations, board members expressed frustration over their relatively passive role and often expressed a desire for more involvement in program policymaking and decision making.

For literacy programs to be effective in a Work First environment, literacy educators will have to develop stronger relationships with outside players. Adult literacy program planners will need to develop collaborative working relationships with various outside groups. Adult literacy practitioners need specific information from representatives of these groups to help them make decisions about curricular content, the skills and knowledge their learners needed, and community resources and opportunities that can augment their instruction. In turn, community agencies and employer groups need to develop a better understanding of the educational mission of adult literacy programs and of how they can contribute to its fulfilment. Developing and fostering these collaborative relationships is a two-way street.

Establishing partnerships will take considerable commitment and work. Partners' paradigms or worldviews may reflect fundamentally different assumptions and values; thus new frames of reference will be needed, representing new and different ways of understanding the other stakeholders. Perspectives that transcend those of each individual stakeholder will need to be adopted. Fortunately, there is a growing body of literature on forming and maintaining partnerships that literacy practitioners can use to guide their efforts in this area. See, for example, Imel (1995a), Molek (1996), Rosenberg (1997), and Rowley and others (1995).

Focusing on Comprehensive Outcomes for Participants. For many years, the success or failure of adult literacy and basic education programs was defined largely in terms of their participation and retention rates. Better programs were defined as those that recruited a larger proportion of their target population and retained a higher proportion of recruited students for longer periods of time. Although these remain critical issues for many adult education programs, workplace development, family literacy, and the demands of Work First welfare policies require a greater emphasis on defining specific knowledge and skills that we want learners to derive from their participation in education and training programs.

Many national studies underscore the need for education and training among adults in basic skills, such as reading, writing and computing. But these studies go well beyond stressing this basic level of knowledge, suggesting the need for a variety of other skills as well, such as interpersonal communication, teamwork, problem solving, critical thinking, and the ability to continue learning on the job. In other words, what is being expected as outcomes of adult literacy programs is being redefined to include not only demonstrable skill in the so-called basics but also skills in an expanded range of other specific outcomes. Although these outcomes are not measured by the GED, they are clearly expected by employers and postsecondary educators alike (Pitts, White, and Harrison, 1999).

Adult literacy practitioners need to work collaboratively with workforce development boards, social services agencies, and educational institutions to better define specific outcomes for their learners. From this effort should emerge a more comprehensive and articulated set of program goals, objectives, and outcomes that represent the efforts of multiple agencies. Within this broader, comprehensive picture, literacy practitioners can better define the outcomes for which they are primarily responsible and the way those outcomes are integrated with those provided by other agencies that serve their students.

Planning and Designing Holistic and Integrated Programs and Curricula. Perhaps the advent of welfare reform has not so much changed the skills taught by adult educators as underscored certain ways of thinking about literacy that have been present for some time. One of the most profound transformations needed in many adult literacy programs is the shift from a view of literacy as a set of discrete, isolated skills to a view of it as a social practice (Fingeret and Drennon, 1997; Grubb and Associates, 1999). When literacy is viewed as a set of discrete skills, individuals are perceived as having a particular facility in reading, writing, and computing, and the purpose of instruction is to enhance these particular skills and abilities. These specific skills are generally construed as a "ladder of competencies" (Grubb and Associates, 1999, p. 145), and student progress in literacy instruction is gradually pictured as moving up that ladder.

Viewing literacy as a social practice locates the notion of literacy and its acquisition beyond the individual learners. It involves the instructor, other students, multiple texts, and the particular social contexts in which literacy is being practiced. From this perspective, learners are encouraged to construct meaning out of their interactions with texts, fellow students, and the instructor.

The view of literacy as a social practice stresses contextual learning and more integrated approaches to curricula. Changing the nature of the curriculum—what is to be learned—will require additional curricular and program planning skills for many literacy practitioners. The curriculum in a Work First environment needs to address students' outside interests and concerns as well as basic skills. Practitioners need to work toward an integration of academic and work-based contexts within the curriculum. They need to shift from a skills-based curriculum to a meaning-making curriculum, one that focuses on practices rather than tasks (Dirkx and Prenger, 1997).

A shift from an academic skills–based notion of literacy to one of literacy as a social practice also requires different instructional approaches. Although we have made great strides in this area, many adult literacy programs continue to reflect highly individualized, workbook-based instruction, organized around learning discrete sets of academic skills. Instructional methods should reflect the inherent social context of learning. This means that practitioners will need to employ more collaborative approaches in their instruction. Curricula need to be reconceptualized in a more integrated and thematic manner (Dirkx and Prenger, 1997), stressing the life contexts and issues in learners' lives, such as their family, community, and workplace settings. Also, adult learners should be more directly involved in all aspects of the program, including program planning and policy implementation.

Developing Systems of Accountability. In the past, participation rates and hours of persistence were often used to assess the effectiveness of adult literacy practices. If they were reaching the target audience and students were staying for a sustained period of time, programs were judged to be performing at adequate levels. Occasionally, GED completion rates were also offered as evidence of program effectiveness.

These indices of performance are increasingly recognized as severely limited in helping us understand the overall effects and outcomes of adult literacy programs, however. In this age of accountability, educators at all levels are struggling to identify and use more appropriate means of assessing the outcomes of their programs. Policymakers and funding agencies are asking what effects these programs are having on students and how they are contributing overall to the needs of the community and society. As welfare reform policy and the Work First environment transform the way adult literacy education is organized and practiced, practitioners will be even more pressed to provide answers to these questions. Many will need to acquire additional knowledge and skill in designing and implementing more holistic and systemic methods of assessment.

Rather than viewing assessment in terms of testing for and documenting the presence or absence of certain skills, we need to understand it within the context of literacy as a social practice. The assessment process should contribute to learners' ability to achieve their educational objectives. Systems of accountability should provide a framework for assessing learning in a holistic sense, provide information on the extent of that learning, and help identify what learning experiences and program features most effectively contribute to it. Results of these assessment processes need to be effectively communicated to the community and outside agencies.

Because of the need to link literacy education with the worlds of work, family, and community, assessment needs to be reframed from a process that is skill-based to one that is more context-based. A business education teacher in a local vocational program recently remarked that one of his learners, who had recently passed the math portion of the GED, was struggling with basic math skills in the context of his vocational course. He was astounded (as was the student) to discover that although the student had passed the math test, he could not perform relatively rudimentary calculations in a work-related environment. The GED is an example of a skills-based assessment process, whereas the observation made by the teacher represents an informal assessment within a particular context. The need reflected by this anecdote is for both instruction and assessment to be grounded in the *practice* of literacy, rather than focusing on discrete, academic skills.

A systemic approach to accountability reflects concern for numerous elements of the assessment puzzle (Dirkx and Prenger, 1997). These elements involve learner, teacher, organizational, and institutional issues. As adult literacy programs reshape themselves within the Work First environment, each of these elements will need to be considered and addressed. More emphasis needs to be placed on procedures of authentic assessment (Schneider and Clark, 1995), such as portfolio development, to assess and demonstrate learner competency. In situations where individuals are preparing for employment, assessment of learning should include a significant component that is work-based. Simulations, such as role plays and standardized employment situations, can also be used to assess learners' readiness in certain areas.

Providing for Continuous Staff Development. Within the last ten to fifteen years, considerable strides have been made in providing training and professional development for adult literacy educators. The constructivist turn in education (Kamii, Manning, and Manning, 1991) has significantly influenced the ways in which we think about and practice adult literacy education. National projects, professional associations, and volunteer organizations have contributed much-needed frameworks, training curricula, and opportunities for continuing education. As a result, many practitioners have developed familiarity with emerging pedagogical practices, content, and materials such as contextual learning, theme-based instruction, technologically mediated instruction, collaborative learning strategies, and authentic assessment.

The Work First environment, however, places new demands on practitioners to acquire additional knowledge and skill. Because of the expanded scope of practice discussed in this chapter and the need for increased familiarity with many specific work contexts, literacy educators must commit to continuous, ongoing continuing education and training. These opportunities should be focused and specific to the particular needs arising from this different environment for adult literacy education.

Conclusion

As we contemplate the transformation of adult literacy education under welfare reform, it helps to remind ourselves of the people at the center of this restructuring. Byron Shaw is one of millions of adults across the globe who on a day-to-day basis lives out the connection between literacy and work that so many of us merely write or read about. As a participant in an American adult literacy program, Byron wrote, "A day without a job is just like any other day, but you don't get paid. Sometimes I wonder if I'll ever find one again. It's crazy getting up in the morning looking for one or two. I hope one comes through. The interviews, the calling, still no answer. Maybe I'll have better luck tomorrow. It's just another day of calling and interviews" (International Task Force on Literacy, 1991, p. 129).

Welfare reform has undoubtedly created a powerful policy context for adult literacy education. This context, more than any preceding policy decisions, promises to fundamentally reshape our notions of practice. Yet as we try to understand and work within this new environment, we must also be thoughtful and critical about the changes demanded of us. Although occupational concerns have always been a core force in adult learning, the field is also guided by strong liberatory, humanistic, and democratizing traditions. Given these traditions, linking adult literacy education with workforce development and welfare reform presents practitioners with a central challenge: How do we continue to foster these aims within our practice while also attending to societal needs for workforce development and welfare reform within an increasingly diverse and technological environment? What do we say to the Byrons of our society? Learning to hold and work with this tension may be the most important skill demanded of literacy practitioners in the Work First environment.

References

Alamprese, J., and Voight, J. *Delivering Family Literacy in the Context of Welfare Reform: Lessons Learned.* Cambridge, MA: Abt Associates, 1998.

Barton, P. E., and Jenkins, L. "Literacy and Dependency: The Literacy Skills of Welfare Recipients in the United States." Policy Information Report. Princeton, NJ: Educational Testing Service, 1995. (ED 385 775)

Cohen, E., and others. *Literacy and Welfare Reform: Are We Making the Connection?* National Center on Adult Literacy Technical Report no. TR94–16. Philadelphia: University of Pennsylvania, 1995. (ED 378 366)

Dirkx, J. M., and Prenger, S. A. *A Guide to Planning and Implementing Instruction for Adults: A Theme-Based Approach.* San Francisco: Jossey-Bass, 1997.

Fingeret, H. A., and Drennon, A. *Literacy for Life: Adult Learners, New Practices.* New York: Teachers College, 1997.

Freire, P. "Cultural Action for Freedom." *Harvard Educational Review,* 1998, *68* (4), 476–521.

Grubb, W. N., and Associates. *Honored but Invisible: An Inside Look at Teaching in the Community College.* New York: Routledge, 1999.

Imel, S. *For the Common Good: A Guide for Developing Local Interagency Linkage Teams* (rev. ed.). Columbus: Center on Education and Training for Employment, Ohio State University, 1995a. (ED 38–88–48)

Imel, S. "Welfare to Work: The Role of Adult Basic and Literacy Education." ERIC practice application brief, 1995b [http://ericve.org/docs/pab00001.htm].

International Task Force on Literacy. *Words Are What I've Got: Writings by Learners from All Around the World During International Literacy Year.* Toronto: Sister Vision Press, 1991.

Kamii, C., Manning, M., and Manning, G. (eds.). *Early Literacy: A Constructivist Foundation for Whole Language.* Washington, D.C.: National Education Association, 1991.

Knell, S. "Learn to Earn: Issues Raised by Welfare Reform for Adult Education, Training, and Work." Washington, DC: National Institute for Literacy, 1998. [http://www.nifl.gov/activities/sknell.htm].

Martin, L. G., and Fisher, J. C. "The Impact of Welfare Reform on the Delivery of Adult Literacy Instruction." In G. S. Wood and M. M. Weber (eds.), *Proceedings of the 1998 Midwest Research-to-Practice Conference on Adult, Continuing, and Community Education.* Muncie, Ind.: Ball State University, 1998.

Molek, C. *Adult Education Community Partnerships: Final Report.* Lewistown, Penn.: Adult Education and Job Training Center, 1996. (ED 40–74–88)

Murphy, G., and Johnson, A. *What Works: Integrating Basic Skills Training into Welfare-to-Work.* Washington, D.C.: National Institute for Literacy, 1998 [http://www.nifl.gov/whatworks.htm].

Pauly, E., Long, D. A., and Martinson, K. *Linking Welfare and Education: A Study of New Programs in Five States.* New York: Manpower Demonstration Research Corporation, 1992.(ED 346 266)

Pitts, J. M., White, W. G., and Harrison, A. B. "Student Academic Underpreparedness: Effects on Faculty." *Review of Higher Education,* 1999, 22 (4), 343–365.

Reder, S., and Wikelund, K. R. *Steps to Success: Literacy Development in a Welfare-to-Work Program.* Portland, Oreg.: Literacy, Language, and Communication Program, Northwest Regional Educational Laboratory, 1994.

Rosenberg, S. "Strategies for Building Local Partnerships." *Adult Learning,* 1997, 8 (3), 21–22.

Rowley, W., and others. "Partnerships for Productivity." *Training and Development,* 1995, 49 (1), 53–55.

Schneider, M., and Clark, M. *Dimensions of Change: An Authentic Assessment Guidebook.* Seattle, Wash.: Adult Basic Literacy Educators Network, 1995.

Sparks, B. "Poor Women's Education Under Welfare Reform." In A. Rose (ed.), *Fortieth Annual Adult Education Research Conference Proceedings.* DeKalb: Northern Illinois University, 1999.

JOHN M. DIRKX is associate professor of higher, adult, and lifelong education and codirector of the Michigan Center for Career and Technical Education at Michigan State University.

Epilogue

Larry G. Martin, James C. Fisher

The social policy link between adult literacy education and workforce development has its roots in the passage of the Manpower Development and Training Act (MDTA) of 1962 (Quigley, 1997). In this act, adult literacy efforts were prescribed for those individuals who lacked a level of literacy commensurate with that required for employment training. This connection was strengthened with the funding of state offices for adult basic education programming in the Economic Opportunity Act of 1964. One purpose of the programs funded under this act was to assist adults with their needs for occupational training. Additionally, when the MDTA was expanded in 1965, it included social policy that linked adult basic education to workforce development (Quigley, 1997).

The recent shift in federal legislation targeting the employment needs of welfare recipients has continued the social policy theme of providing employment opportunities for impoverished adults; yet, adult literacy programming is not a central component of the new legislation. Armed with various studies investigating the effects of academic programs on the employment prospects of low-literate welfare recipients, policymakers have rendered suspect the role of adult literacy programs in helping welfare recipients find and maintain employment. Consequently, adult literacy programs have been challenged to demonstrate their worth by proving that increased employment opportunities accrue to welfare recipients who participate in them.

This challenge questions the current organization and implementation of adult literacy education programs. For example, can a system of state-operated programs with an administrative core of a limited number of full-time administrators, an instructional staff of generalist part-time teachers, and a cadre of volunteers provide the types of programming and services required to help the entire range of welfare recipients acquire and retain employment? Can programs with curricula that target the academic skills required for a high school degree best help welfare recipients acquire employment in the least amount of time? Can literacy programs continue to operate with limited funding from state and federal sources and effectively serve the educational and employment needs of the country's most impoverished adults?

The contributors to this sourcebook suggest that literacy practitioners need to rethink their profession to align it with the demands of the new Work First environment, identify a more specific niche in the education of welfare recipients, and meet their own pragmatic expectations. First, the legislative agenda is still in flux, and practitioners must not only understand existing law but also actively seek to shape the outcome of proposed legislation. Second, as practitioners experiment with alternative approaches to programming, instructional methodology, and delivery systems, research and evaluation should take center stage, and the results should be made available to policymakers. Third, the welfare-to-work effort has resegmented the target population of out-of-school low-literate learners. Therefore, alternative curricular approaches should be employed with specific types of former and current welfare recipients, such as those with learning disabilities. Fourth, employment-based programs should use the context of the workplace to maximum benefit in the literacy education effort. Fifth, community-based programs should plan their efforts to more specifically target welfare recipients if such students will continue to attend their programs. Sixth, program staff and administrators should be continuously involved in staff development and training to provide them with the knowledge, skills, and attitudes required to lead their programs during this period of rapid and complex change.

Reference

Quigley, A. B. *Rethinking Literacy Education: The Critical Need for Practice-Based Change.* San Francisco: Jossey-Bass, 1997.

LARRY G. MARTIN *is associate professor of adult and continuing education and department chair at the University of Wisconsin-Milwaukee.*

JAMES C. FISHER *is associate professor of adult and continuing education at the University of Wisconsin-Milwaukee.*

INDEX

Back Issue/Subscription Order Form

Copy or detach and send to:
Jossey-Bass Inc., Publishers, 350 Sansome Street, San Francisco CA 94104-1342

Call or fax toll free!
Phone 888-378-2537 6AM-5PM PST; Fax 800-605-2665

Back issues: Please send me the following issues at $23 each.
(Important: please include series initials and issue number, such as ACE78.)

1. ACE _____

_____

_____

$ _____ Total for single issues

$ _____ Shipping charges (for single issues *only;* subscriptions are exempt from shipping charges): Up to $30, add $5^{50} • $30^{01}–$50, add $6^{50} $50^{01}–$75, add $7^{50} • $75^{01}–$100, add $9 • $100^{01}–$150, add $10 Over $150, call for shipping charge.

Subscriptions   Please ❏ start   ❏ renew my subscription to *New Directions for Adult and Continuing Education* for the year _____ at the following rate:

❏ Individual $58   ❏ Institutional $104
NOTE: Subscriptions are quarterly, and are for the calendar year only. Subscriptions begin with the spring issue of the year indicated above. For shipping outside the U.S., please add $25.

$ _____ Total single issues and subscriptions (CA, IN, NJ, NY and DC residents, add sales tax for single issues. NY and DC residents must include shipping charges when calculating sales tax. NY and Canadian residents only, add sales tax for subscriptions.)

❏ Payment enclosed (U.S. check or money order only)

❏ VISA, MC, AmEx, Discover Card #_____ Exp. date_____

Signature _____ Day phone _____

❏ Bill me (U.S. institutional orders only. Purchase order required.)

Purchase order #_____

Name _____

Address _____

_____

_____

Phone_____ E-mail _____

For more information about Jossey-Bass Publishers, visit our Web site at:
www.josseybass.com   **PRIORITY CODE = ND1**